JUSTICE FOR CHILDREN

JUSTICE FOR CHILDREN

Centre for the Study of the Child & Society
University of Glasgow

in collaboration with
UNICEF (UK) and Save the Children Fund (UK)

edited by

Stewart Asquith and Malcolm Hill

MARTINUS NIJHOFF PUBLISHERS
DORDRECHT / BOSTON / LONDON

Library of Congress Cataloging-in-Publication Data

Justice for children / Centre for the Study of the Child & Society,
  University of Glasgow, in collaboration with UNICEF (UK) and Save
  the Children Fund (UK) ; edited by Stewart Asquith and Malcolm Hill.
        p.   cm.
    Based on the proceedings of the International Conference on
  Justice for Children, held at the University of Glasgow, Sept. 1992.
    Includes bibliographical references and index.
    ISBN 0-7923-2645-8 (HB : acid-free paper)
    1. Children--Legal status, laws, etc.--Congresses.   2. Children
  (International law)--Congresses.   3. Child welfare--Congresses.
  4. Children's rights--Congresses.   5. Children--Legal status, laws,
  etc.--Scotland--Congresses.   I. Asquith, Stewart.   II. Hill,
  Malcolm.   III. University of Glasgow.   Centre for the Study of the
  Child & Society.   IV. International Conference on Justice for
  Children (1992 : University of Glasgow)
  K639.A55   1992
  346.01'35--dc20
  [342.6135]   93-42894

ISBN 0-7923-2645-8

Published by Martinus Nijhoff Publishers,
P.O. Box 163, 3300 AD Dordrecht, The Netherlands.

Sold and distributed in the U.S.A. and Canada
by Kluwer Academic Publishers,
101 Philip Drive, Norwell, MA 02061, U.S.A.

In all other countries, sold and distributed
by Kluwer Academic Publishers Group,
P.O. Box 322, 3300 AH Dordrecht, The Netherlands.

Printed on acid-free paper

Printed in the Netherlands

CONTENTS

2

ACKNOWLEDGEMENTS

The conference which yielded this publication was organised in collaboration with UNICEF (UK) and Save the Children Fund (UK) and the help of Gill Wilcox and Alison Davies respectively extended the international appeal of the conference and lead ultimately to this book. For her usual patience, forebearance and good humour in producing the final manuscript many thanks are due to Laura Lochhead of the Centre for the Study of the Child & Society.

In a book of this size it was only possible to include the presentations by the main speakers at the conference and we would like to thank the contributors for speedy responses to tight deadlines and to adapting the spoken material to written form, sometimes necessitating work in a second language. Unfortunately, the other contributions at the forty-five workshops during the conference could not be published. Alternative means of publishing some of these have been found but we would here like to acknowledge the importance of those other papers to the success of the conference.

The book would not have been possible without the support, encouragement and patience shown to us by Lindy Melman of Martinus Nijhoff and we would like to thank her for that.

Notwithstanding the contributions made by those mentioned above, any mistakes are entirely our responsibility.

Stewart Asquith and Malcolm Hill
University of Glasgow

CONTRIBUTORS
(in alphabetical order)

Stewart Asquith: St Kentigern Professor for the Study of the Child and Director of the Centre for the Study of the Child & Society, University of Glasgow, Scotland.

Donald Duquette: Clinical Professor of Law and Director, Child Advocacy Law Clinic, University of Michigan Law School, USA.

Thomas Hammarberg: Director of Radda Barnen, Sweden, and member of the UN Committee on the Rights of the Child, Sweden.

Malcolm Hill: Senior Lecturer in Social Policy & Social Work and Deputy Director of the Centre for the Study of the Child & Society, University of Glasgow, Scotland.

Savitri Goonesekere: Professor, Faculty of Humanities and Social Sciences, The Open University of Sri Lanka, Sri Lanka.

Andrew Lockyer: Lecturer in Politics, University of Glasgow, and former Chairman of Strathclyde Panel Members, Scotland.

Gary Melton: Carl Adolph Happold Professor of Psychology and Law and Director of the Center on Children, Families and the Law, University of Nebraska, Lincoln, USA.

Theresa Penna Firme: Professor and Dean of Graduate School of Education, Federal, University of Rio de Janeiro, Brazil.

Richard Reid: Director, Division of Public Affairs, United Nation's Children's Fund., New York.

John Triseliotis: Professor of Social Work, Department of Social Policy and Social Work, University of Edinburgh, Scotland.

Nyorovai Whande: Women and Children Officer, United Nations High Commissioner for Refugees, Geneva, Switzerland.

INTRODUCTION

Stewart Asquith and Malcolm Hill

This book is based on the proceedings of the **International Conference on Justice for Children** held at the University of Glasgow in September 1992 and organised by the Centre for the Study of the Child & Society in collaboration with Save the Children Fund (UK) and UNICEF (UK). The conference was held to mark the 21st anniversary of the unique system for dealing with children in Scotland known as the Children's Hearings System and had four main aims.

Firstly, the conference was conceived not simply to commemorate the 21 years of the Children's Hearings but also to examine critically their operation in the context of broader international issues.

Secondly, in December 1991, the UK had ratified the United Nations Convention on the Rights of the Child though with a number of reservations relating largely to the Children's Hearings in Scotland. The conference was then to afford the opportunity to examine the implications of the convention for the lives of children not just in Scotland and the UK but from an international perspective drawing on the experiences of a number of countries from the wider international community. The UN Convention heralded a new era in the social, political and economic status of children and it is inevitable that there will be change required in the way we as adults deal with and relate to children as members of the community, as parents or as professionals employed in our major social institutions such as law, education, social work and health.

Thirdly, the conference was to allow for the exchange of ideas and information between researchers, practitioners and policymakers from different countries. From the outset, the intention had been that the conference would be attended not by members of one particular constituency whether it be research or practice or policy making, but that the delegate membership would be drawn from all of these. The philosophy underlying the conference was that there was a need for greater dialogue not simply between those from different countries but also between all those with a particular interest in children.

Fourthly, the conference was to be concerned with the notion of "justice for children" and more specifically with a conception of justice more akin to social justice. With the coming social and political changes required by truly implementing the principles of the UN Convention on the Rights of the Child, the concept of justice as it relates to how we treat our children throughout the world has to embrace more fully notions of equity and fairness. And by being child centred , such a concern requires that attention be focussed on not just how children are dealt with by legal institutions and within particular countries but also more importantly on the status and respect that is afforded to them worldwide as human beings.

Almost 300 delegates from around the world attended the conference, representing very different constituencies and professional groupings, and from a range of countries including Barbados, Sweden, the Netherlands, Germany, Uganda, Brazil, Vietnam, Sweden, Kenya, Hong Kong, Canada, USA and of course the UK.

The conference was held over a three day period and as well as the plenary sessions there were over 45 workshops on a range of themes and topics. The presentations at the plenary sessions provide the basis of this edited book.

JUSTICE FOR CHILDREN IN SCOTLAND

Given that the conference was conceived to mark the 21st anniversary of the Children's Hearings system in Scotland, we present a summary of the main principles on which the system is based and describe some of the key features of this unique approach to dealing with children who commit offences and/or who are in need of care and protection.

But before doing so, some comments on the social and legislative differences between Scotland and England will be made- and this is important for any attempt to understand the Hearings system. Such a comparison is necessary to underline the fact that though both Scotland and England are part of the United Kingdom, there are major social and institutional differences between both countries. In particular, as we shall see, Scotland has retained a separate legal system and whereas historically England has generally been associated with a traditional form of juvenile court, Scotland has never had a systematic, uniform juvenile court structure, a fact which in part accounts for the development of a radical form of juvenile justice in the 1960s. But the need for such a comparison also reflects our belief that to understand adequately any juvenile justice system, the philosophy on which it is based has to be related to wider issues about the society in which it is located.

Politically, at the time of writing Scotland has diverged from much of the rest of the UK, with only 11 of the 72 Scottish members of parliament belonging to the party of government. The education system is also distinct from the English one with different philosophies, structures and qualifications. This applies both to schools and universities and the breadth of the Scottish educational experience is seen to derive from a more European and particularly, French, philosophy.

Similarly, the legal system is very different and many of our procedures and positions again have wider European roots. There is a radically different system of juvenile justice. In relation to children generally, because of the separate legal and juvenile justice systems, when the UK signed the UN Convention on the Rights of the Child in December 1992, there were certain exclusion clauses which did not apply to Scotland. For example, article 37 states the right of the child to prompt legal or other assistance - the difficulty with that for Scotland is that there is no legal representation in the children's hearings system.

It is impossible to understand the development of juvenile justice in Scotland without understanding something about the development of social work - indeed the two go hand in hand. In Scotland, local authority social work departments carry out all aspects of social work including probation, parole and work with offenders - there is no probation service in Scotland. This can be compared with England where not only is there a different system of juvenile justice but there is a separate probation service. What this means is that all social work with offenders, young and old alike, is carried out by social work departments alongside all their other responsibilities such as child protection, community care, work with the elderly, disabled and mentally ill people. Not only are there such wide responsibilities but some of the social work departments are large, paradoxically for a small country like Scotland with a population of around 5 million are large and Strathclyde is the largest single social work authority in Europe serving a population of over 2,200,000.

The significance of discussing the social work department is that the present structure of social work was introduced by the same piece of legislation which introduced the Children's Hearing system - the 1968 Social Work (Scotland) Act on the basis of which the Hearings were implemented in April 1971.

THE KILBRANDON REPORT AND THE CHILDREN'S HEARINGS IN SCOTLAND

In April 1992, the Scottish Children's Hearings System had been in operation for 21 years. Since its introduction the general acceptance of the Hearings as an appropriate forum for the making of decisions about children has been reflected in the absence of any vigorous or concerted arguments either in favour of its abolition or in rejection of the philosophy on which it is based. This is despite the fact that it introduced a radical and unique system of juvenile justice and justice for children -the two go together in that the Children's Hearings system, as we will see is not simply a justice system designed to deal with children who commit offences. Rather it is a system of justice for children in which the welfare of the child is the key concern.

There have of course been changes introduced and questions asked about both the practice and the philosophy underpinning the Hearings System during the past 21 years, and that is only to be expected. By and large, however, any alterations to the system have been mainly incremental either by way of extension to its remit or in the form of practical attempts to provide solutions to the tensions and conflicts experienced by most systems of juvenile justice. The whole question of children's rights, a key element throughout the conference, and the extent to which the rights of children are protected within the Children's Hearings System, can only benefit from a consideration of how such issues are seen in the rest of Europe and the rest of the world.

The Children's Hearings system is based on the philosophy of justice for children advocated by the Report of the Kilbrandon Committee (Kilbrandon 1964). Though the recommendations contained in the Kilbrandon Report were seen to be radical and controversial at the time, they provided, with some modifications, the philosophical basis of the 1968 Social Work (Scotland) Act. It took only four years from the publication of the Kilbrandon Report in 1964 to legislative provision for the introduction of a revolutionary form of justice for children, rejecting traditional notions of how to conceive of and deal with children, particularly children who commit offences. As we pointed out above, Scotland never had a traditional juvenile court structure as did England and other countries but had a range of different types of courts in which children who committed offences could appear. The implication of this is that not only was there no history of a strongly rooted juvenile court structure but there was also no organised and politically powerful body of juvenile magistrates as there had been in England. This may in part have accounted for the lack of opposition to what, for a country steeped in Calvinism, were radical proposals for dealing with those who committed offences.

The Kilbrandon Committee had been appointed in 1961:

> 'To consider the provisions of the law of Scotland relating to the treatment of juvenile delinquents and juveniles in need of care and protection or beyond parental control and, in particular, the constitution, process and procedures of the courts dealing with such juveniles, and to report.'

What had made the recommendations of the report so controversial was the rejection of a court based system of justice as inappropriate for children. A second major assumption underpinning the main recommendations of the report was that there was no essential difference between children who commit offences and children in need of care and protection. (Martin, Fox and Murray 1981; Asquith, 1989).

The basic conflict for any system of juvenile justice is how best to reconcile the competing claims of the law, judicial process and punishment with the need to take into consideration the welfare of children. The Kilbrandon Committee had argued that delinquency or offence behaviour should be seen as symptomatic of need and that children who commit offences should be dealt with in the same way and in the same forum as other children in need of care and protection.

The committee had also recognised that any court system which has to take into consideration the responsibility of offenders and can punish, is inhibited when it comes to making decisions about the most appropriate welfare measures for children. A court based system was rejected therefore:

> - because of the impossibility of reconciling the determination of guilt with welfare dispositions,

> - because of the inappropriateness of punishment for the majority of children who offend;

> - because of the inappropriateness of having welfare decisions made by those who have the expertise and training to decide on questions of guilt or innocence but who lack the necessary expertise when it comes to the needs of children;

> -because court proceedings themselves were seen to prevent open discussion and the opportunity for full exploration of the needs of children. The formality and ritualistic nature of court proceedings was seen to militate against the best interests of the child in so far as they prevented open and informal discussion, and had the potential to stigmatise.

The Kilbrandon philosophy is one in which justice for children means providing appropriate measures to help children and their families, and the very operation of the system has to be judged by different criteria. There are obviously issues that have to be fully resolved in terms of procedural guidelines. Nevertheless, the Children's Hearings system has been in the forefront of juvenile justice systems in promoting a conception of children's rights which include giving children the right to be heard, to be involved in decision making about their lives, and to be treated with decency and respect in a system that is ultimately concerned with their well being (Fox 1991). In that respect, the Children's Hearings anticipated many of the conditions laid out in the Convention on the Rights of the Child. And despite the commitment in a number of countries to the juvenile court structure, the Children's Hearings continue to attract international interest as a possible model for future reform (Fox 1991). They also share principles with other European systems. In France, for example, the separation of criminal and civil jurisdictions - the separate treatment of those children who commit offences from other children in need of care and protection is unacceptable (Garapon 1989).

As a unique solution to the basic conflict of the juvenile court, the Kilbrandon Committee had recommended the complete separation of responsibility for deciding on guilt or innocence from the responsibility of deciding upon appropriate welfare measures. It is this principle which is the foundation stone on which rests the Children's Hearings System as introduced through the 1968 Act and implemented in April 1971.

To sum up, the main principles on which the Hearings system is based are:

(i)   The welfare of the child is the key factor in all decisions
(ii)   Delinquency is symptomatic of need
(iii)   The only criterion for intervention is the need for compulsory measures of care
(iv)   Children who commit offences should be dealt with by the same body as deals with children in need of care and protection

The Kilbrandon Committee also believed that the judiciary lacked the skills needed to make decisions about children. In all cases, decisions about children's welfare, whether of children who offend or children in need of care and protection, are ultimately the responsibility of three members of the community, the **panel members**, whose **only** remit is to make decisions about the need for compulsory measures of care. There are 1700 panel members in the whole of Scotland and their distribution reflects the diverse sizes of the country's local authorities. For example, in Strathclyde there are 800 panel members, more than half the national figure. In Orkney, one of the island authorities there are 13.

The 1968 Act had also created the post of **Reporter**. It is to the Reporter that all initial referrals are to be made, and he or she has the discretion to decide whether or not a case should proceed to a hearing. The Hearings themselves are not courts of law and the only issue which the panel members can rightly concern themselves with is whether the child appearing before them is in need of compulsory measures of care.

It is well nigh impossible in such a brief commentary to give a comprehensive picture of the Scottish Children's Hearings system and in any case Andrew Lockyer in Chapter 9 gives a fuller statement. Nevertheless, it is clear that there are a number concerns which have to be considered about any system based largely on a philosophy of welfare and the Children's Hearings system is no exception. What was apparent from the discussions at the conference is that such concerns are being examined in relation to other jurisdictions, some of them striking at the very basis of welfarism as it applies to children.

For example, there is some concern at the absence of legal safeguards for children in the Hearings system and that insufficient protection is being afforded to their rights. Similarly, and closely related, is the danger that there may be too much discretion in the system available to key personnel.

Such concerns have been around since the introduction of the system and have been the subject of continuing comment. Nor are they of purely conceptual interest for they have significant implications for the actual functioning of the system in practice, as events over the past 21 years or so have shown. They all relate to the key question that has to be asked of any system of juvenile justice. That is, the extent to which a system based on welfare principles and concerned ultimately with the best interests of the child can at the same time offer children and their families protection from unwarranted interference, abuse and intervention in their lives from the very system designed to help them.

Any system of justice for children has also to be seen in the context of the social, political and economic climate in which it is located. Over the past two decades there have been important shifts in political ideology in the UK (some of which do not fit easily with a system based on welfare principles); there have been significant changes in social work thinking about how to deal with children; the economic situation has changed considerably; there have been a number of dramatic occurrences involving the deaths of children, some of whom have actually been in public care; physical and sexual abuse have been" discovered"; and the very citizenship status of children and their rights have become common currencies in the political agenda. This shows again that no understanding of a system of justice for children can be adequate if it ignores the social, political, economic and historical context in which it is located. This has a number of general implications.

One is that the justice of a system of juvenile justice has to be assessed not simply in terms of the procedural correctness in which decisions affecting the lives of children are made. Rather, the justice of that system has to be appreciated in relation to the social and economic circumstances in which children find themselves. A conception of rights which was exclusively concerned with the legal rights of children and ignored their broader social rights would have to be fundamentally questioned. For example, the changing structure of family life in Scotland and the increase in the number of children experiencing poverty have both to be taken into consideration in determining the justice of how we treat our children.

Another, is that we have to acknowledge that the preoccupations with the rights of children will take very different forms in different countries. The concentration on children's rights **within** systems of justice, which has been a preoccupation of Western industrialised communities is in stark contrast to a conception of the rights of children in third world countries where basic survival is an issue or where children are subjected to the rigours and consequences of war. More specifically, until recently the conception of rights promoted for children in the West has been largely that of children's legal rights (See for example, Morris and Giller eds 1983). Children's legal rights are of course important and there is no argument being made here to the contrary. But where legal rights are divorced from a consideration of more substantive social rights and social justice, then concern has to be expressed about the adequacy of such a conception of rights for children.

Similarly, recognition has to be given to the fact that the promotion of rights for children in one country will depend to a great extent on the political and economic strategies of others. It is inevitably a truism but, as was discussed often during the course of the conference, the experiences of children and the extent to which their rights *qua children* are respected are inextricably linked to the vagaries of world economies.

In adopting the Convention on the Rights of the Child, the United Nations established a framework of minimum standards which could be adopted in all countries but which would require to be implemented and realised with reference to the peculiarities of national differences.

UN CONVENTION ON THE RIGHTS OF THE CHILD

The rapid social and demographic changes which children have experienced in the last decade have been accompanied by gradual but continuing alteration to their social and political status. In particular, the United Nations Convention on the Rights of the Child embodies a whole new philosophy which will influence current and future developments relating to children.

By ratifying the Convention, governments are committed to the full implementation of the rights set out in the Convention and which can be grouped into three broad categories:

Protection: children have a right to protection from cruelty, abuse, neglect and exploitation
Participation: children have a right to play an active role in society and to have a say in their own lives
Provision: children have a right to have their basic needs met

By granting children (all those under 18) universal rights, the convention at the same time places children's issues on the political agenda and also puts them in an international context. Moreover, the universality of the rights granted through the convention means that children should not be discriminated against on grounds of age, gender, ethnicity, religious affiliation or class.

The convention is based on the philosophy that children are equals and that they have the same value as adults. But they are also at the same time vulnerable because of their age and because of the ways in which their lives are subject to the decisions and behaviour of adults. Herein lies a tension, not just for the Convention but for adults either as parents or as members of agencies responsible for children - how best to treat children as equals but at the same time recognise their vulnerability. Two articles in the convention are crucial in this respect. Article 3.1 states :

> In all actions concerning children, whether undertaken by public or private social welfare institutions, courts of law, administrative authorities or legislative bodies, the best interests of the child shall be a primary consideration.

Thus, the interests of others including parents and social work, education or health agencies are less important than those of the child. As we saw, this is a crucial aspect of the Scottish Children's Hearings System.

Moreover, the child should also have a say in decisions about his or her future. Article 12.1 states that:

> States Parties shall assure to the child who is capable of forming his or her own views the right to express these views freely in all matters affecting the child, the views of the child being given due weight in accordance with the age and maturity of the child.

What these articles reflect is the view that the protection of children has to be balanced with a concern for their growth to independence and respect for their rights as individuals. The Convention, far from establishing a framework which would allow children to do simply what they wanted, relates rights to responsibilities. Children are to be offered protection when needed but are also to be given greater opportunities for participation in and exercising responsibility over decisions affecting their lives as and when appropriate. The right of children to their childhood, particularly younger children, is protected against excessive demands imposed by the expectation that they should behave as adults.

One of the main implications of the Convention is that developments in child care and child law will increasingly give children the right to be involved in decisions in all situations in which they find themselves whether these involve their parents or other adults in key agencies such as health, social work or education.

Though the Convention is child centred it should not be seen as only commenting on the rights of children. It also states the rights, responsibilities and duties of parents and legal guardians. The right of parents and legal guardians to provide "appropriate direction" in the exercise of rights by children is qualified again by the need to recognise the importance of children's interests and the evolving capacities of the child. In fact the Convention embodies the principle that separation of the parents in no way absolves either parent from the responsibility of parenting. Parents and the family are to be given support and assistance but when it is clear that children are not being given sufficient protection or help to express their wishes then the state has to intervene, with the child's interests a primary consideration.

Moreover, the Convention imposes obligations and duties on states to provide the material and other wherewithal necessary for children to realise their physical and intellectual potential. For example, Article 27 states that:

> States Parties recognise the right of every child to a standard of living adequate for the child's physical, mental, spiritual, moral and social development.

> States Parties....shall take appropriate measures to assist parents and others responsible for the child to implement this right and shall in case of need provide material assistance and support programmes, particularly with regard to nutrition, clothing and housing.

Broadly speaking what the convention does is not simply set up a list of rights for children and impose a correlate set of duties on others such as parents and the state. It goes further than that in presenting a framework whereby the very social and political status of children, their relationship to their parents and adults in general may be viewed very differently. It alters the balance of power between children and adults in such a way that children generally can play a more active part in democratic social life. It also imposes duties on states to provide the necessary resources with which children can grow to realise their potential and can themselves contribute to social and political change throughout the world.

Ultimately, a concern with justice for children says something about how they are conceived of as members of society and also mirrors the very notion of justice we as adults employ. Perez de Cuellar put it neatly when he said

> The way a society treats its children reflects not only its qualities of compassion and protective caring, but also its sense of justice, its commitment to the future and its urge to enhance the human condition for coming generations. This is as indisputably true of the community of nations as it is of nations individually (quoted in Flekkoy 1991)

THE CONTRIBUTIONS TO THIS BOOK

The Conference was organised in such a way that the presentations fell into one of four broad, overlapping themes. These were (i) the UN Convention and the universality of children's rights; (ii) Models of Justice; (iii) Children in the Community; and (iv) Separated Children.

In Chapter 1, Richard Reid discusses the significance of the UN Convention on the Rights of the Child in creating a mechanism for global change in the way children are treated. The articles of the Convention itself introduce important principles on which to base radical change in the lives of many children throughout the world whether they be in Scotland, Bosnia or Somalia. Moreover, he asserts, such change could be aided by and should exploit the global communications network through which people everywhere can be sensitised to the appalling circumstances in which many children find themselves.

In a similar vein, **Gary Melton** in Chapter 2, considers the plight of children on the world stage arguing that at such a critical juncture in world history, a reduction in human suffering is within reach through political and technological reform. There is however no guarantee that this will come about. In particular, the restructuring of the world order could well overlook the needs of children and their promised social and political integration into their communities.

The doubt expressed by Melton is challenged by **Thomas Hammarberg** in Chapter 3 in his review of the political and other developments leading up to the adoption of the Convention by the United Nations. Whereas the Convention lacks the support of meaningful sanctions for those who fail to implement the articles, it has nevertheless become a powerful mechanism for change in the lives of children and has sensitised the world community to the need to address the philosophy on which adults, in their many roles, relate to children. Children's rights and needs have been placed firmly on the international and political agenda.

Savitri Goonesekere argues in Chapter 4 for the acknowledgement of children's rights as universal and rejects what she refers to as a relativist position whereby rights and justice can vary according to the social, religious and political differences of countries throughout the world. Only on the basis of universal norms and standards will the spirit of the UN Convention be realised in imposing duties on people throughout the world to adopt the same standards and practices towards children.

In Chapter 5, **Nyorovai Whande** considers the plight of refugee children, arguing that it is impossible to speak about such children apart from their mothers. The experiences of refugee children are inextricably linked to the experiences of women and mothers. Refugee children, she asserts, are in double jeopardy because they are children and because they are refugees. It is a terrible indictment on the world that in many instances the situation of refugees and refugee children in particular could be eased with the adoption of very simple and low cost measures.

In Chapter 6, **Theresa Penna Firme** discusses the position of street children and points out the importance of involving children and young people in the movements and organisations which promote change. A policy of inclusion is needed in relation to young people whose lives may be characterised by deviant values and life styles so that social and political changes occur which genuinely improve their life opportunities.

Whereas Penna Firme's arguments are derived from her experience in Latin America, **John Triseliotis** in Chapter 7 addresses the problem of the experiences of children in residential institutions in Eastern Europe, particularly in Romania. Though there are obviously common factors in the development of policies and frameworks for dealing with children separated from their parents, there can be less certainty that the historical legacies of different countries are the same. With specific reference to residential child care in Romania, Triseliotis considers the implications of the historical trends there before examining the types of infrastructures necessary to promote radical change and hopefully improvement in the conditions in which children find themselves.

The representation of children and the protection of their rights within a system of justice is central to debates about the development of appropriate justice systems for children. And in relation to the UN Convention as saw above, it is in this respect that the UK registered reservations for Scotland when ratifying the Convention. **Lockyer** in Chapter 8 and **Duquette** in Chapter 9 develop the debate on the need for representation for children in the Scottish Children's Hearings system. Though the context they both refer to is specifically Scottish the issues they raise are general and have wider implications for discussions about how best the rights of children might be protected within a system of justice. Lockyer, after reviewing the philosophy of the Scottish Children's Hearings, argues that there is no need for a new individual such as a child advocate to be appointed and that to do so would introduce yet another official into the system for children to deal with. In contrast, Duquette, drawing on the experience in the USA of Court Appointed Special Advocates argues that the Children's Hearings system in Scotland would benefit greatly from the introduction of "Child Advocates" . The child advocate would look after the rights of the child, promote his/her best interests and generally guide the child or young person through the whole process of involvement with a major social institution such as the Children's Hearings system. Moreover, the introduction of the Child Advocate, Duquette suggests could be done without in any way threatening the integrity of the system.

A common theme which pervades all the contributions in this book and which links the diverse papers given at the workshops during the conference was the need to see the concept of justice in much broader terms than simply the adherence to formal rules and regularities. This is not to deny the importance of due process and natural justice within systems for dealing with children. But in itself is not enough. The justice of a system or institution which ignores the way in which life opportunities are distributed and ignores the fact of basic inequalities in the social and economic opportunities afforded to certain groups in society has to be questioned. Similarly, from an international and moral point of view, a world in which different categories of people are discriminated against in terms of gender, religion, race or age cannot be considered just. With specific reference to children, the justice of the ways in which we deal with children does not simply illustrate what seem to be appropriate forms of relationship between children and adults. It goes further than that by indicating what we take justice to mean in the first place.

REFERENCES

Asquith, S. (1983) *Children and Justice* Edinburgh University Press

Flekkøy, M. G. (1991). *A voice for children: Speaking out as their Ombudsman.* London: Jessica Kingsley.

Fox, S. (1991) *Kilbrandon Child Care Lecture*, University of Glasgow

Garapon, A. (1989) *Child Representation in the French Child Care System* Ecole Nationale de Magistrature, xerox

Kilbrandon Report of the Committee on Children and Young Persons (Scotland) Cmnd 2306 HMSO, Edinburgh

Martin, F., Fox S. and Murray (1981) *Children Out of Court* Scottish Academic Press, Edinburgh.

Morris, A, and Giller, H (eds) (1983) *Providing Criminal Justice for Children.* Edward Arnold, Londond.

CHAPTER 1

CHILDREN'S RIGHTS: RADICAL REMEDIES FOR CRITICAL NEEDS

Richard Reid

Rights are an explosive topic. Generally it is rights, and the question of how they are to be acknowledged or parcelled out, that demarcate the dividing line between social philosophies -- between political parties. Wars have been fought over rights; most revolutions have begun with perceived rights abuses as the prime cause.

It is adult rights -- the debate, struggle, and bloodshed associated with adult rights -- that I have just referred to. Defining and securing them has been difficult enough; it has taken more than 200 years of blood and strife to acknowledge the basic unanimity expressed in the Universal Declaration of Human Rights. But when these rights were fully spelled out in 1948, few if any thought of children as anything but corollary beneficiaries. The children would, it was assumed, be sheltered by the rights of the adults. That should cover them sufficiently. And this, by and large, was the conventional wisdom that prevailed in the world through the early Eighties.

So there is now something quite radical in the idea of children's rights and the way they are spelled out in the two-year-old Convention on the Rights of the Child. It is radical because it enfranchises a whole new cohort of population -- a restless, original cohort seldom expressly sheltered by any important body of rights or law before. It is a cohort which, in its pre-adolescent childhood, is regarded at best with fond patronisation by the general public; in its adolescence and teenage ranks, it is regarded with widespread uneasiness and even fear. All those of us who support the Convention on the Rights of the Child and wish to see it implemented must take stock of these public feelings, and must realise that we are entering a sociopolitical "radioactive zone" when we discuss the categories of children's rights that go beyond the familiar consensus-supported areas of health, education, and protection from war and violence. Essentially the 54 articles of the Convention boil down to what one might call "the three P's" -- protection, provision, and participation. The first two, protection and provision, are comfortable enough. It is the experientially uncharted third P, participation, that causes the yellow caution lights to flash on. What kind of participation? How much? At what age? Won't it derange the social order?

There was an element of the radical, certainly, in the adoption 21 years ago of the Scottish Children's Hearing system. The System not only emphasised the welfare of the child, but rejected the idea of the child as <u>object</u> of protection or care. Rather, the child became a <u>subject</u> with rights very like those of adults.

The Children's Hearing System promoted the idea that children have the right to be heard, to be involved in decisions that affect them. This conception preceded by more than a decade the basic principles of the Convention on the Rights of the Child. Let me just cite for you some provisions of the Convention that provide a strong legal basis for the child's participation.

Article 12, for example, says that governments "shall assure to the child who is capable of forming his or her own views the right to express those views freely in all matters affecting the child, the views of the child being given due weight..."

And, it continues: "For this purpose, the child shall in particular be provided the opportunity to be heard in any judicial and administrative proceedings affecting the child ...".

Article 13 guarantees the child the right to "freedom of expression". This right includes "freedom to seek, receive and impart information and ideas of all kinds, regardless of frontiers...."

And Article 14 recognises the child's right "to freedom of association and to freedom of peaceful assembly."

Bodies of law designed to protect from painful trespass a minimum roster of humankind's basic entitlements <u>have</u> served to challenge the status quo, provoke introspection, and incite action -- but only recently. The Universal Declaration of Human Rights was promulgated in the 1950s, but lay dormant -- the '50s and '60s were not ripe years for Rights -- until the mid-1970s.

Amnesty International and other human rights groups saw the possibilities. Their agitation, their purposeful action, made people living under oppression -- the tortured, the imprisoned, people under dictators -- aware of their rights. From Moscow to Chile, from South Africa to Poland, a clamour went up. People demanded an end to the damage being done to them by dictatorships. Change stirred in Central and Eastern Europe, soon in other regions.

The human spirit was primed for an age of complementary actions that would summon international consensus on a set of basic freedoms and dignities to which all of humankind is entitled by birth, transcending as they do the purviews of governments or individuals, and -- most critically important and historically remarkable -- design and ratify a process to implement and then guarantee the stewardship of those human rights. Such a process was set in motion by the adoption in 1989 and ratification in 1990 of the Convention on the Rights of the Child -- a process that promises steadily increasing social justice for children in the not-distant future.

An important advance made by the Convention on the Rights of the Child is the elevation of the traditional category of children's essential <u>needs</u> to the category of <u>rights</u>, codifying them along with the responsibility of society to ensure that they are respected. It stresses "the best interests of children" while rejecting, at the same time, all forms of discrimination based on gender, race, colour, language, or religion. It merges, for the first time, civil and political rights on the one hand, and economic, social, and cultural rights on the other, treating this broad range of rights as an indivisible whole.

One hundred and twenty-two countries have ratified the Convention as of today. And built into the treaty they signed is a means of gauging the seriousness with which the governments are taking up their commitment to their nation's children. Governments must report, within two years of ratification, on how they are following up on the Convention. They report to a group of six women and four men, ten eminent persons from ten different countries, experts on rights, child development, and the law. These experts comprise the Committee on the Rights of the Child, elected by States Parties and set up to monitor how effectively countries are implementing the treaty. To one degree or another, <u>all</u> countries -- industrialised and developing -- have problems fulfilling their responsibilities to children and can benefit from international support in working to correct them. UNICEF is working closely with governments in all parts of the world, at their request, in the Convention follow-up process and, as mandated in the treaty itself, with the Committee on the Rights of the Child.

The Committee has not been content to sit and wait for reports to arrive. They have begun taking the Convention on the Rights of the Child to the people -- to the children themselves.

Recently in Quito, Ecuador, the Committee became the first UN body responsible for human rights to travel as a group into the countryside of a developing country, coming in touch with the conditions whose change they are charged with monitoring, and imparting to the people in the region they visited a sense of the vibrancy and potential of the Convention. Ecuador was the right setting for this first field trip, underscoring as it did one of the most important attributes of the Convention: children's participation. Two years ago, Ecuador's children voted in a referendum on the Rights of the Child -- some of those children participated in the Committee's June meeting in Quito.

One 14-year old concluded a brief but riveting speech to Committee members, saying: "When we participated in the diagnosis for the Great Agreement we said that our schools don't teach us properly: education relies a lot on rote learning. Schools also discriminate against working children and against native children. We have campaigned to get the teachers to recognise their mistakes, so they can correct them. The police mistreat us a lot," he went on. "We have carried on a lot of campaigns with them. As you can see, we are defending and disseminating our rights. With your assistance we can achieve our goal; please help us defend our rights."

An iron string of continuity runs from the unanimous adoption of the Convention by the United Nations General Assembly in November 1989 through its coming into force as an international treaty in September 1990 (upon the ratification by a national government) and up to the use, around the world throughout 1992, of the Convention as an ethical reference point by a rising chorus of voices speaking against the victimisation of children in such war areas as Somalia, Bosnia, Sudan, Mozambique, and Afghanistan.

The Convention, which took ten long years to work its way through the United Nations machinery, became international law almost with the speed of light, less than a year after it was adopted by the General Assembly. And in an orchestrated parallel opportunity during that same month, the World Summit for Children turned out to be the common denominator around which the leaders of East and West, North and South -- 71 heads of state and government and senior officials from another 88 countries -- could meet for the first time. The challenge now is for us to maintain the synergy between the Convention and its implementation through the World Summit for Children Declaration and Plan of Action.

The signatories to the World Summit Declaration and Plan of Action began the process by first agreeing on the principle that children's basic needs must be given a "first call", or priority, on society's resources, in good times or bad times, in war and in peace. Second, the world leaders agreed on a strategy for making this principle operative, complete with measurable goals, a time frame for achieving them and mechanisms to monitor progress along the way. They committed themselves to meeting 27 goals by the year 2000, an agenda for action -- an agenda in every way compatible with the Convention on the Rights of the Child.

Upon the foundation of the Convention, more than 120 governments are now in the process of formulating their "National Programmes of Action" -- a process important in itself because it involves government ministries, a broad scope of organisations and elements of society, the mass media and, as in Ecuador, children themselves. In mid-1992, the Secretary-General reported through ECOSOC to the General Assembly on the status of progress in all countries, and on the drawing up of National Programmes of Action, region by region, toward the Summit goals (and therefore toward many Articles of the Convention.) Following the path of progress, a decision made by UNICEF mandates that all new country programmes be based on and integrated with the Convention. By the end of 1992, that path led us to reports to the Committee on the Rights of the Child being due from the first 57 ratifying countries on their implementation of the Convention.

The synergistic interplay between an international treaty (the Convention) and specific country programmes (the National Plans of Action) gives promise of achieving rights for children in realistic ways -- within each nation, during a measured time frame. But on the streets and in the villages of country after country, the world is now showing itself to be a dangerous and violent place where conditions increasingly menace children more than any other group in the population. The most lethal of these conditions draw our attention to protection and provision --categories of rights still absolutely unavailable to a large fraction of the world's children today.

Nearly thirteen million of these children die every year --some 36,000 a day. The numbers stun the mind. How is this possible at a time of radically expanding immunisation and diarrhoea control by the health services of even the poorest countries? The answer is that malnutrition and disease have been reinforced, especially over the past two decades, by a powerful multiplier agent: <u>armed conflict</u>. And it is the principal reason many of these children have had no vaccines and oral rehydration -- or sufficient food. In World War I, only a tenth of the casualties were civilian; now, 90 percent of those who die due to war are non-combatants, particularly children. In the Sudanese civil war up to mid-1989, it was estimated that 14 children died for every dead government soldier or rebel.

A glance at the world's mortality tables is instructive. The first, second, and third highest child mortality rates in the world are those of countries whose names are synonymous with war --Mozambique, Afghanistan, and Angola. Roughly a third of the young children in these countries do not live to see their fifth birthdays. Close behind them are Ethiopia, Somalia, Liberia, and Cambodia. A measure of the size of child losses in these countries is that they are occurring at a constant rate probably five times greater than Bosnia's.

The Somalias and Bosnias of today were prefigured in the past by some wars that fell squarely on civilian populations, but never on the scale that is the norm now, and not with the frequency. Historically, there ran a sense, approaching a taboo, that children were beyond the limits of attack. State-sponsored conflict took place mainly on battlegrounds well away from towns and settlements. And added to this was the aura of near-holy innocence attached to children until the start of this century. They were God's image. In earlier eras they were also revered as the seed-corn of the race, insurance against extinction. Population replenishment was crucial. And so, across hundreds of generations, there emerged a social contract that bound combatants to protect and spare children and the defenceless.

That contract began to lose its adhesion with the advent of mechanised war and has pulled apart more and more rapidly since. At this moment, there would appear to be no contract at all on the ground where the fighting rages, no shield worth the name for children and the defenceless, only ceasefires and safe passages that evaporate at a gunman's whim.

With the Convention on the Rights of the Child as our moral compass and National Plans of Action as our guides, we must match with strong new protections the pace and capacity of armed conflicts to kill, stunt, and maim our children. At the least we must insist that a protective cloth be cut from the pattern of four different cases of humanitarian intervention, carried out between 1985 and 1991 in four different countries--El Salvador, Lebanon, Sudan, and Iraq--during four different wars. We must insist that the pattern followed during those conflicts -- a pattern in which warring factions ceased their fire to allow for the enactment of critical, if temporary, interventions for the children -- should become the blueprint for standard procedure. World adherence to "days of tranquillity" for life-saving interventions like immunisation, "corridors of peace" through which food and basic commodities can travel unimpeded, safe havens and shielded respites from gunfire that restore the bare minimum measure of protection to children in armed conflicts: we must catapult the definition of such interventions from modern-day phenomena to the level of accepted practice -- and from there to minimum acceptable practice in times of war. An agreement was also reached in Bosnia-Herzegovina for breaks in the fighting to allow provisions to reach families and children.

Now, with a Convention in place, and as each day creates new victims in need of its shelter, moral norms and levels of outrage have risen. Forces supporting the Convention on the Rights of the Child are exacting a strict application of its armed conflict protection articles: they demand adherence to such basic international standards as those spelled out in the Convention's Article 38, which protects children under 15 from taking direct part in hostilities, and calls upon States Parties to take all feasible measures to ensure protection and care of children who are affected by an armed conflict; and compliance with the provisions guaranteed in Article 22, which calls for the humanitarian assistance and protection of children defined as refugees and those seeking refugee status.

Rights are upon us; we have harnessed ourselves into a commitment to honour the rights of humans and children, and nine-tenths of the world has signed the agreement.

But had we loitered over these past very decades -- had the Convention on the Rights of the Child and National Plans of Action never existed to form the framework in which we all plan and build -- today's changed conditions and expectations would have forced us to improvise just such a framework.

Perhaps traceable to the first full strides of the communications revolution, the genesis of a demand for children's participation was inevitable. A world that brings adults face-to-face, minute by minute, with children -- a world, in fact, that less and less frequently draws the line between adult and child --cannot ignore its younger citizens' humanity, and with that their human rights to the expression of opinions, and to the fora that will allow them appropriate levels of influence in decisions made for them or in spite of them.

The other characteristic of our modern times that would have propelled the world into improvising <u>protections</u> for its children, with or without a Convention, is the preponderance and the hideous reality of today's wars -- a reality that has moved with horrifying speed from sporadic, to episodic, to the now constant fact of armed conflicts marring every corner of the map, exposing the defenceless -- mainly children -- to unprecedented harm.

It is self-preservation that impelled us toward an international treaty of protections, provisions, and participation for our children. We humans -- that most vulnerable of species --have evolved into a breed of forward-thinkers to protect ourselves from our own kind. We looked ahead and saw a day in which a majority of children in some regions -- especially, but not exclusively, older children -- would be emotionally, socially, and politically atrophied by non-participation, while others in other regions -- another obscenely large percentage -- would lie ripped and bloodied or traumatised and dispersed in the crossfire of adult conflicts.

The Convention on the Rights of the Child offers a vehicle for creating a world conscience that speaks on behalf of children. The global communications revolution furnishes a first-time opportunity for sensitising people everywhere to the reality of life for too many of the world's children, and to the rights they ought to be entitled to exercise: protection, provision, participation.

Provision will be the least complicated of the elements of the Convention on the Rights of the Child to implement, and the most straightforward to arrange for within a National Plan of Action. The other two sets of rights -- participation and protection -- will demand the very best of us. Only when our most tactful persuasive powers are brought to bear will general public support tip in favour of the radical notion of children as participants. And only when indignation is given a knife-edge of urgency -- to the point we would reach in watching our own children tortured and killed -- will we shake ourselves free of the disgrace of children in war.

The fact of the global village means that the luxury of indifference to such suffering is gone forever. Like it or not, we are our brothers' keepers -- and guardians of his children.

CHAPTER 2

IS THERE A PLACE FOR CHILDREN IN THE NEW WORLD ORDER?

Gary B. Melton

DEVELOPMENT OF A NEW WORLD ORDER

We live in extraordinary times. In 1989 at the fortieth anniversary of the Fulbright programme in Norway, I heard a Hungarian academician begin his keynote address by proclaiming that the one thing that the United States had that Hungary did not was a Communist party. In November 1991, I visited the Union of Soviet Socialist Republics - a nation that a few months before my visit had enough military power to destroy the world and a few weeks after my visit had ceased to exist. Meanwhile, South Africa has taken the first steps to end apartheid, and it has begun to reenter the world community - a shift symbolised by its entry of an integrated team into the Olympics. A new government in Israel moved immediately and fervently toward reconciliation with its Arab neighbours--less than two years after some of those countries welcomed the arrival of missiles on Israeli soil, and others joined a nearly worldwide alliance against the country that launched the missiles. (After this sentence was written, Israel raised new concern with its forced expulsion of hundreds of Palestinians into southern Lebanon.) A decade ago dictatorships reigned in most of Latin America; today democracies have sprouted in most countries in the region. The list could go on.

At the same time, we are reminded how fragile those momentous changes are. Just a couple of months before I visited Moscow, tanks had roared through its streets. Although people had been triumphant in turning back the military machine, eyes that had "glistened with hope" - a phrase used by one of my hosts - too often seemed to have become dull with disillusionment. On the same trip that I visited the USSR, I visited the beautiful historic city of Prague and noted the excitement in restoring the vibrant Czech culture and building a political system that was responsive to the needs of the citizenry. I was impressed by more serious, better informed discussions with government officials than I have experienced anywhere else in the world. Today that government has been toppled by ethnic conflict -a tragedy that pales in comparison with the atrocities occurring every day in former Yugoslavia. Meanwhile, war threatens to erupt again in the Persian Gulf, and violence continues in South Africa while people of colour continue to be effectively excluded from the political process. Just as the list of positive changes is long, the list of threats to sustained movement toward protection of human rights could go on.

Perhaps the most vivid illustration of the limits of democracy's triumph were the riots in Los Angeles. In words that probably were penned months before that disaster occurred, Marian Wright Edelman (1992) eloquently stated the dilemma facing the nation:

> Ironically, as Communism is collapsing all around the world, the American Dream is collapsing all around America for millions of children, youths, and families in all racial and income groups. American is pitted against American as economic uncertainty and downturn increase our fears, our business failures, our poverty rates, our racial divisions, and the dangers of political demagoguery. (p. 81)

I suspect that the dramatic movement toward democracy that we have witnessed is irreversible. In the analogue to the legal economists' claim that the law moves inevitably toward efficiency (Landes & Posner, 1987), I have hypothesised that, at least in democracies, the law develops in the direction of support for human dignity (see, e.g., Melton, 1992, 1993). Nonetheless, our euphoria at the end of the cold war and the substantial reduction in the risk of nuclear annihilation is balanced by our anguish as we witness continuing violence - localised but brutal hostilities, even in our own land - and by our anxiety about the uncertainty that lies ahead as the gap between privileged and impoverished continues to widen, both at home and around the world. We live in a time of new hope but also new Angst.

With so much spectacular change, to say that we are at a critical juncture in human history is almost trite. Whatever the political overtones that accompany the term, it seems inevitable that we are entering "a new world order." Although a permanent reduction in human suffering is not a fait accompli, political reform and technological advancement have combined to put that goal within reach, perhaps for the first time in history. The challenge is to avoid the risk that global restructuring will create new divisions among people and harden old lines that keep some from enjoying a decent standard of living in conditions that promote their dignity.

CHILDREN IN A TIME OF CHANGE: SOME PERSONAL IMPRESSIONS

A POLITICAL TRAVELOGUE

The momentous opportunities and the accompanying risks that the community of nations now faces are paralleled by equally striking developments and possibilities in the reformation of the status of children around the world. The opening is present for the creation of societies that keep their promise, made by leaders around the world in 1989 and 1990 that children will share in the "recognition of the inherent dignity and of the equal and inalienable rights of all members of the human family" and that they will be "brought up...in the spirit of peace, dignity, tolerance, freedom, equality, and solidarity" (Convention on the Rights of the Child, preamble, 1989; see also Detrick, 1992; Grant, 1992; World Declaration, 1990). At the same time, risk is present that children's special needs and concerns will be overlooked or ignored as the world is configured anew--that children will lack a place in the new world order.

My personal anxiety about the future for the children of the world has been shaped by a series of remarkable experiences that I have had in the past few years. Those experiences have left me with vivid impressions about the challenges that lie ahead if the promise of full integration of children into the global community is to be kept. I take the liberty of taking readers on a verbal, admittedly somewhat egocentric travelogue of my meanderings, both geographic and intellectual, because they provide a context for directions -both positive, even utopian, and negative, even catastrophic -that we may take from the crossroads before us. The images are disparate; they sum, though, to a complex picture with an important, relatively consistent message.

LESSONS FROM NORWAY

As a Fulbright professor in Norway, I had the opportunity to interview scores of public officials, researchers, and advocates about various child and family issues and, in particular, to assess the effectiveness of the office of the ombudsman for children, a Norwegian innovation (Melton, 1991; see also Flekkøy, 1991). I was struck by the speed with which the ombudsman's office had become a part of the culture.

I also worried, though, about the sense of crisis in child and family welfare that was prevalent even in an affluent country with a highly developed, popularly accepted social welfare system. In action that seems sadly familiar on this side of the Atlantic, during one of my visits to Norway the ombudsman for children brought charges against public officials in three municipalities for failure even to investigate reports of suspected child maltreatment. Indeed, when I have presented the report of the U.S. Advisory Board on Child Abuse and Neglect (1990) that proclaimed a national emergency in the American child welfare system, the reaction not only in Norway but throughout northern Europe has been that, except for the depiction of the scale of the problem and the contribution of poverty to its prevalence, the description of an emergency applies as well to their own child protection systems.

In examining the process of formulation of child and family policy in Norway, I was surprised to find an absence of influential advocacy groups to guard the interests of children. Indeed, I became convinced that the holes in the social welfare system were primarily the lack of effective grassroots action, not only in the political arena but also in everyday life in neighbourhoods (cf. Gullestad, 1984, 1991).

When a country has undergone rapid urbanisation and even more rapid change in family life (the situation, as I shall discuss, in most developed countries), development of a safety net of social, economic, and health services is important, but it is not enough. The notion that people need people (more precisely, that families need social support) is not simply the romantic fantasy of a songwriter (Thompson, 1992). When traditional sources of social support become largely inaccessible or simply unavailable, other sources of ongoing support are necessary to help families in dealing with everyday crises. By their nature, highly professionalised and bureaucratised services are unable to meet that need. Services are most likely to be effective when they are flexible--when they are delivered in "natural" settings like the home and the school, and when they are not confined to measured units of service (e.g., fifty minutes of psychotherapy) but instead are delivered when and where people need them (Henggeler & Borduin, 1990; Melton & Hargrove, in press). Unfortunately, though, in Norway as in other developed Western nations, the typical response to family change has been simply to increase office-based services, not to take steps to weave a new social fabric.

The result is that there is a widespread sense of crisis, "reflected in a common belief that the state no longer can be relied upon to provide a social safety net with holes too small for children to fall through" and in support, even among previous opponents, of special agencies or organisations to advocate on behalf of children. There also is recognition even in welfare states that "significant gaps remain on the 'cradle' side of 'cradle-to-grave' social welfare" (Melton, 1991, p. 230), gaps that have widened as a result of demographic and economic change.

THE ISRAELI SITUATION

Although many Norwegian children may be said to be in danger, the menace is subtle. Norway is still in the process of urbanisation; accordingly, social networks have not yet stabilised to meet new residence patterns (Flekkoy, 1991; Statistisk Sentralbyrå, 1992). Although overall mobility does not yet approach the American level, 1 in 3 five-year-olds has experienced a move of home. At the same time, Norway, like other developed countries, has had substantial changes in its divorce rate, which doubled between 1970 and 1987, and its rate of births outside marriage (now 39%). Meanwhile, the economic status of two-parent families and, even more so, single-parent families has declined to a point that it is, on average, substantially less than childless couples. Accordingly, Norway faces the social risk that accrues when traditional social supports and structures weaken, especially when that tatter in the social fabric is further strained by "exceptionally difficult conditions," to use the polite language of international law and politics (Convention, 1991, preamble).

In some instances, though, the threats that children experience are more immediate and powerful than the perils that accrue when there are simple mismatches between the social ecology and children's needs. Sometimes the hazards of life are so great that they threaten the survival of children and their families, and the fear that results preoccupies parents and children and motivates withdrawal or aggression. At other times, the level of hatred and mistrust that exists threatens the psychological integrity of people on both sides of the mirror image and consumes the energy that is available for productive activity (cf. Bronfenbrenner, 1961; White, 1977).

Although an American need not go abroad to find examples of the situation that I am describing (DeAngelis, 1991; Garbarino, Dubrow, Kostelny, & Pardo, 1992; Garbarino, Kostelny, & Dubrow, 1991; Youngstrom, 1992), I was profoundly moved by a visit to Israel a few weeks before the Gulf War began. I participated in a symposium on the rights of children that was sponsored by the Israeli chapter of Defence for Children International (Freeman & Veerman, 1992)--the only international meeting that was held in Israel between the time of the Iraqi invasion of Kuwait and the end of the Gulf War.

During that visit, our group discussed child protection issues with leaders of Jewish family agencies. At a meeting with lawyers and counsellors providing support to Palestinian youth, we listened to moving, often horrible stories of work with youth in East Jerusalem and on the West Bank--many of whom had been injured in the Intifada or confined in terrible conditions (see Veerman, 1991) and all of whom had been excluded from school for lengthy periods. We had lunch in the home of a leader of the Druze Arabs in a town near Haifa--a home that combined a traditional Arab lifestyle with decorations consisting of pictures of American and Israeli warplanes. We met with the council of the Church of the Annunciation in Nazareth--one of the holiest sites in the Eastern Orthodox Church--and heard about the social welfare programmes that they had developed for Christian Arab families and youth.

These meetings were complemented by wildly contrasting images, as an account of a single day illustrates. We began one day by visiting the Children's Memorial at Yad Vashem (the Holocaust museum in Jerusalem), a beautiful, haunting memorial in which recitation of the names and ages of children murdered during the Holocaust takes place in total darkness other than that provided by the mirrored flicker of candles. Outside the Memorial, we saw a number of young Israeli soldiers (presumably on leave) preparing to enter the Memorial; all had Uzis strapped to their shoulders. From Yad Vashem, we went to Tel Mond, a youth prison, where we saw Jewish youth in quadruple-bunked cells and Arab juveniles--described by the prison superintendent as political prisoners (cf. Veerman & Samaan, 1992) - in physical conditions at least as bad but with only one hour a day out of their cells for exercise.

From Tel Mond, we visited the lush estate of a family of aristocratic British Jews, who had bought the estate just after the Six-Day War. Prior to that time and the subsequent annexation of the Occupied Territories, the strip of Israeli land on which the estate is found was only a few miles wide. The previous owner had abandoned the estate after the family's gardener was murdered by a terrorist in their yard.

The day ended on Mount Carmel with lighting of a Chanukah candle at Yemin Orde, a resettlement school for 500 unaccompanied juvenile immigrants--many of whom were Ethiopian Jewish youth who for the first time were being formally introduced into Jewish culture and religion.

The impressions that were left that day were so striking that the contrasts alone were unsettling (apart from the fact that what we had seen often was disturbing in itself), especially when placed in the disquieting, somewhat eerie context of high security and deserted tourist attractions and hotels. The visual contrast between beauty and atrocity was less stark, however, than the contrast of perceptions among the groups with whom we visited.

Regardless of ethnicity or religion, adult leaders described with considerable poignancy the anxiety that their own families and their clients' families experienced on a daily basis. The risk that war in the Persian Gulf would spread to Israel seemed somewhat remote at the time, in part because people were preoccupied with more immediate perils: seemingly random outbursts of violence that had intensified since the then-recent Temple Mount massacre; economic threats, posed especially but by no means exclusively to the Arab minority, by the extraordinary influx of immigrants from Eastern Europe, the precipitous drop in tourism, and the worst drought in many years.

Nothing was as troubling to me, though, as the attributions that were made about the ultimate cause for a situation in which fear forms a part of everyday life. For example, the Christian Arab leaders in Nazareth--highly educated, mostly middle-aged or older men who gave no appearance of radicalism--suggested that Iraq's invasion of Kuwait was for the purpose of showing the world what an occupation is like, and that the result would be a significant improvement in the lives of Arabs in Israel and the Occupied Territories. Jewish groups tended to attribute their anxiety to the threat of Arab violence; Arabs attributed their anxiety to political and economic oppression. Youth programmes on the West Bank that conceptualised their work as psychosocial rehabilitation found that the occupying forces regarded such efforts as "recycling terrorists"; the military acted accordingly and periodically raided their programmes.

I was left with the impression that everybody was right and everybody was wrong and that there was no common ground on which negotiations could be built (cf. Bar-on, 1991). In a short time, though, the political context has changed substantially. With the rearrangement of alliances in the Gulf War, the removal of the Soviet Union as a force in the region, and the change in government in Israel, the possibility of significant movement toward a lasting peace is real. No one should be misled, though, into thinking that the process will be easy or that hostilities cannot reemerge or even deepen.

It is clear that children have the most at stake in ensuring that change is positive. The Intifada is to a large extent a children's war; youth throw the stones and bear many of the casualties (Garbarino et al., 1991). In fact, one research group conducting a study on the West Bank was unable to find *any* children in some towns who had not been shot, detained, arrested, beaten, or tear gassed. The school is the community institution that has been the focus of the most intensive military action in the Occupied Territories (Lewis, 1991). In a situation that in some ways parallels our own, Israeli children and families bear the brunt of high defence spending (Passell, 1992)--a situation exacerbated by the high cost of assimilating recent immigrants from Eastern Europe (Lief et al., 1991). Perhaps most fundamentally, children--regardless of their ethnicity--are apt to be most harmed by a daily life in which their parents and often they themselves live in fear, which periodically escalates into sheer terror (Garbarino et al., 1991; Greenbaum, 1991).

THE SITUATION IN EASTERN EUROPE

Although nothing may match armed conflict in the threat that it raises to personal security, the ambiguity that is attached to rapid political, economic, and social change brings its own anxiety. In that regard, the change in Eastern Europe offers the potential for substantial improvement in the quality of life of the people living there, but it also brings considerable risk, especially for children, even in those countries in which change so far has been peaceful.

To understand the current situation, it is useful to consider the trends that prevailed in Eastern Europe before the countries in the Soviet Union's sphere of influence began to break away and the Soviet Union itself broke up. Perhaps the most telling fact is that life expectancy, which was always lower than in the West, had been on a steep fall since the 1960s (Castle-Kanerova, 1992; Deacon, 1992; Deacon & Vidinova, 1992; Mezentseva & Rimchayevskaya, 1992; Manning, 1992; Millard, 1992; Ministry of Health, 1990; Mission, 1991; Szalai & Orosz, 1992). In general, the quality of life was steadily declining - a fact that the Gorbachev government recognised but could do little to reverse.

Unfortunately, the welfare of children has plummeted further, as resources have declined, social disorganisation has increased, and much of the pre-existing network of social and health services has been abolished or simply has disintegrated (see Melton, 1991a), as planners have lacked the time, foresight, expertise, or hard currency to create a new safety net and to replace Marxist family codes (see Melton, 1988). Poverty has been rising rapidly (see, e.g., Deacon, 1992; Grant, 1992). As the price of food has skyrocketed, child nutrition has declined accordingly. Russian sociologists regard poor nutrition and other problems of public health as among their two or three most serious problems at present (Melton, 1991a, remarks of Vladimir I. Markov). Research in 1990 by the Research Institute of Mother and Child in Warsaw showed that 80% of schoolchildren did not drink a glass of milk each day, and fewer than one-fifth ate a full meal at school each day (Ministry of Health and Social Welfare, 1991).

Meanwhile, the new governments have lacked the resources to repair the ever-worsening threats to child health left by the industrial policies of the previous governments and complicated by current attempts to decentralise the economy (Deacon, 1992). Pollution is widely acknowledged to be an extraordinary problem in Eastern Europe. For example, public health officials in Poland estimate that 95% of the surface water in that country is contaminated, a problem that has been exacerbated by the recent marketing of Western infant formula as an alternative to breastfeeding (Melton, 1991a, remarks of Malgorzata Grzemka). Health professionals in Eastern Europe believe that the high level of pollution--of which the Chernobyl fallout is the most glaring example--is probably responsible for high rates of birth defects and developmental problems, but epidemiological studies are only beginning (Kalish, 1993).

The result of the declining standard of living in combination with the poor system capacity is that standards of child health continue to plummet (Grant, 1992). The Czech Ministry of Health, recently described the situation, "without exaggeration, as *a chronic and deepening crisis of health and health care in our country* (Ministry of Health, 1990, p. 4, emphasis in the original).

Not only have children's health and welfare declined, but the services needed to remediate such problems have been jeopardised. Expenditures for services to children have actually been declining (Grant, 1992), and shortages of supplies and gaps in technology are resulting in poor-quality care in many places in Eastern Europe.

For example, in a visit to a major paediatric teaching hospital in Moscow (Melton, 1991a), administrators indicated that, in part because of humanitarian aid from the West, that hospital (unlike those in more remote areas) had adequate supplies. Physicians in our delegation, though, noted that much of the medical technology being used was decades out of date by Western standards. Children in the intensive care unit were being injected frequently because of a shortage of tubing for intravenous administration, and even complex surgery was being conducted with local anaesthesia. The surgical suite and the wards had tile floors with grout cement, thus making sterile conditions nearly impossible. The patient areas were old-style wards without adequate facilities for parent stays.

In the naïve belief that a market strategy would eliminate such problems, health care professionals in Eastern Europe with whom I have talked have uniformly looked to private insurance as the answer to their problems of health care delivery--a response that probably would amuse American policy makers struggling to find a feasible programme of health care reform. The lack of trained health care administrators--indeed, the lack of anyone who ever has managed a billing system--indicates the difficulty of the task ahead.

Apart from the formidable technical, fiscal, and human-resource problems, UNICEF officials have observed "signs that the baby of minimum welfare measures is being thrown out with the bath water of state control" (Grant, 1992, p. 18). Because of their aversive experience with intrusive state action, Eastern Europeans now are understandably reluctant to establish new public service systems and regulatory mechanisms.

Nowhere is this ambivalence more acute than in the field of child protection. On the one hand, health and welfare officials (unlike the previous regime) recognise the reality of child abuse and neglect. On the other hand, they lack experience in either managing or participating in a child protection system, and they are sceptical about the desirability of state action in this regard. The result is that Eastern European countries generally lack even the rudiments of a child protection system. It is significant that a recent UNICEF-sponsored review of child protection efforts in numerous countries, including several developing nations, failed to include a status report from any countries in Eastern Europe (Daro et al., 1991).

The dispositional alternatives available in cases of child maltreatment, which are seldom identified in any event, are typically limited in practice to either no action at all or jail for the offending parent and placement of the child in an orphanage (Himes, Kessler, & Landers, 1991; Melton, 1991a). In the current political and economic crisis, the uncertainties about even this narrowly circumscribed system were illustrated by the comment of the director of an orphanage in Moscow that she did not know the budget for the following day (Melton, 1991a).

The length of the path to be travelled in developing a child protection system in Eastern Europe was epitomised by an editorial in *Child Abuse and Neglect*. In that editorial, Richard Krugman (1990) told the following story about the pre-*glasnost* view of child maltreatment in Eastern Europe:

> Several years ago at the First European Conference on Child Abuse and Neglect in Rhodes I met a Romanian minister who shook his head as he heard of the large numbers of children in the US, Western Europe, and other parts of the free world who were abused and neglected. I asked him if there was any child abuse in Romania. "No," he said, "we have none." "Really? I wonder why that is?" I asked. "In Romania," he told me, "we have no child abuse because it is against the law!"
>
> Suppressing an urge to exclaim, "I wish we'd thought of that," I pushed forward. "Do you have any problems with prostitution? Murder?" "Yes," he admitted. "We have some of that, but not as much as in your country." "Well, you must have abuse, then," I said. "In our experience, nearly all prostitutes have been sexually abused as children, and nearly all our murderers have been physically and often sexually abused as

well." He fell silent for a moment, then said, "All our prostitutes and murderers are gypsies. None of them are Romanian." (p. 299)

Although consideration of the problem of child maltreatment was greater in former Czechoslovakia than in other Eastern Bloc countries (Dunovsky, 1991; cf. Kordacki, 1991), identification of child maltreatment "is still a vision of the future" even there (Dunovsky, 1991, p. 5), and a comprehensive system of response is a more distant hope. The authorities in the previous regime suppressed study even of fatalities (Dunovsky, 1991).

The new governments have some appreciation of the range of social problems affecting children; they do not deny, for example, that child maltreatment exists and that it may be worsening because of the political and economic uncertainty and hard times. Perhaps because of the intellectualism in the Czech government, it has been particularly sensitive (relative to other former Eastern Bloc nations) to the "people problems" ahead (see, e.g., Havel, 1992).

Even in the Czech Republic, however, few appreciate the psychosocial issues that they are likely soon to face. For example, mental health professionals with whom I spoke did not understand the potential problems when parents deal with adolescents who have many more choices available than the parents did at the same age (Melton, 1991a). More fundamentally, neither policy makers nor the general public in Eastern Europe seem to recognise the need to transform parent-child and teacher-pupil relations if they ultimately are to socialise people into democratic values.

Some of the psychosocial challenges ahead have never been faced elsewhere, because they relate to the cultural changes that were products of policies of the previous regime. Although many recognise the need to build individual initiative and to enhance worker productivity and care, there are more subtle problems related to family life. For example, because people were required to share housing, regardless of their desire for privacy, households became something other than conventional families as they are defined in the West or, historically, Eastern Europe (Deacon, 1992; Manning, 1992). With the additional complicating factor of the need to establish that one is an heir to pre-World War II owners in order to obtain private ownership of the home, boundaries of the family now are subject to dispute.

Housing policy also has resulted in cultural changes in reproductive behaviour. With children being the means for a couple to obtain their own apartment, the mean age of first childbearing has been about seven years younger than in the West, and the mean age of first marriage also has been several years younger (Dunovsky, 1991; Melton, 1991a, remarks of Alena Kroupova). In former Czechoslovakia, 80% of young couples lived initially with their parents; five years later, 20% still did. One-half of all married women were pregnant at the time of marriage (Kovaik, 1991). Moreover, the distortions that housing policy created in "natural" family life cycles were complicated or exacerbated in many instances by population policy.

The Romanian policies that prohibited contraception and abortion--and the abandoned children and atrocious orphanages that resulted--have received much attention in the West. Although the disregard for family planning was most severe there, the general problem was present throughout Eastern Europe (see, e.g., David, Dytrych, Matejcek, & Schuller, 1988). Contraception continues to be poor in quality and often unavailable (Melton, 1991a, remarks of Kate Schechter, Aleksey V. Geraskin, and Mikhail Schneiderman).

In summary, although the resurgence of democracy in Eastern Europe offers exciting possibilities, it also has dramatically increased the already substantial risks to children, and changes of social and political structure needed to mitigate those risks have been slower to occur. To a large extent, the task is no less than one of rebuilding society, particularly those institutions like the family that are crucial to children's development.

Although the opportunities (and the risks) are immense, so far there has been little attention by either political leaders or social scientists (whether they are based in Eastern Europe itself, the West, or international organisations) to the development of new social support systems and new ways of relating at an individual level. There are some glimmers of hope, however. For example, voluntary and religious organisations are being formed to assist in care for children (Dunovsky, 1991). New youth organisations--or in some instances, pre-existing organisations that have come "above ground"--also may help. The enthusiasm for such developments is illustrated by the fact that eighty thousand boys had joined Scout troops in Czechoslovakia alone by the end of 1991 (Melton, 1991a). The safety net must be expanded and woven more tightly, though, if children are to reap the benefits of political freedom in Eastern Europe.

A NATIONAL EMERGENCY IN CHILD PROTECTION

The examples that I have used so far have been from abroad. The greatest proportion of my time since 1989 has been spent, though, in activities related to the U.S. Advisory Board on Child Abuse and Neglect (of which I have been a member since its inception). Nothing in my professional life has been so exhilarating or so maddeningly frustrating. The experience has been virtually paradigmatic of the theme of this Article: the problem of child maltreatment has reached a point of crisis, the opportunities are present for fundamental change, but the obstacles are formidable.

Just as in the other examples that I have presented, the response in the United States to the crisis in child protection has been mixed, and the future is both worrisome and unclear. No one can doubt that the problem is one of catastrophic proportions--disastrous in its scope, its impact, and the failure of a multi-billion dollar system that is on the verge of collapse (U.S. Advisory Board on Child Abuse and Neglect, 1990).

The numbers are stunning: growth from an estimate of 300 cases of battered child syndrome in 1962 to 60,000 reports of suspected maltreatment in 1974 to 1.1 million in 1980 - a number that more than doubled in the 1980s (U.S. Advisory Board, 1990). As problems of the children entering the system have become increasingly serious and complex and resources have failed to increase at anywhere near the rate of increased cases, there has been a precipitous increase in the number of children in foster care while the number of foster homes has declined. By the middle of the decade, it is estimated that there will be five hundred thousand foster children, most of whom have significant emotional, behavioural, and educational problems, in fewer than one hundred thousand foster homes (National Commission on Foster Care, 1991) - numbers that by themselves indicate the seriousness of the crisis.

As the Board began to grapple with the state of the nation's response to the threat to children's safety, we developed a problem list that went into the hundreds before concluding that (1) the system was in such horrible shape that the declaration of a national emergency was justified and (2) the roots of the crisis were inherent in the system and could not be fixed simply by increasing expenditures to a level proportionate to the increase in cases. Those conclusions did not come easily; many hours were spent in sometimes emotion-filled discussions within the Board and with various professional associations and other interested groups.

Our frustration and conflicts seemed to be based on the fact that the child protection system had lost - or perhaps never found - a sense of mission. The child protection system had mysteriously lost any real focus on the needs and experiences of children (U.S. Advisory Board on Child Abuse and Neglect, 1991). Instead, investigation, seemingly for its own sake, seems to drive the system. "Child protection" seems to have become defined as the work of Child Protective Services (CPS), the unit of state and county child welfare agencies that is charged with investigating reports of suspected child maltreatment - a unit that has become an increasingly large part of social service agencies.

As a result, other sectors of society that should be involved in the prevention and treatment of child abuse and neglect (e.g., health, mental health, schools, churches) typically do not see those functions as important parts of their work, and "child protection" consists of little more than checking off boxes. Workers spend their time gathering or reporting evidence about whether parents did or did not engage in particular conduct, whether pre-adjudication (in determination of whether a report is founded) or post-adjudication or post-disposition (in determination of whether court jurisdiction can be continued or parental rights terminated) - not in planning or delivering services to strengthen troubled families or help maltreated children. At the same time, as CPS and foster care have become the centrepiece of child welfare services in many states, a suspicion of maltreatment ironically and tragically has become a de facto eligibility requirement for receipt of family services.

The lack of attention to children's needs in individual cases is mirrored in - and probably the result of - errant public policy. When child abuse was "discovered" in the early 1960s, it was believed to be an atrocious but rare problem that would be alleviated if only it came into public view. Accordingly, all states adopted mandatory reporting laws, and the focus of both state and federal policy became encouragement of health and human service professionals and the public at large to report suspected child maltreatment to CPS (Nelson, 1984).

Consistent with that focus, the central question of child protection policy became, "Under what circumstances is coercive state intervention justified?" That question leads policy to focus on procedures for evidence gathering and admission, the clarity of the definition of child abuse and neglect, and so forth. By contrast, the central inquiry ought to be, "What can government and society as a whole do to prevent harm to children?" The latter question leads logically to development of support systems that minimise the need for disruption of families and that go well beyond the CPS agency or even the specialty child welfare system to make child protection a part of everyday life.

The Board concluded that the nation needs a new national strategy guided by a comprehensive neighbourhood-based, child-centered child protection system, and it proposed--amid an expansive blueprint for federal involvement--adoption of a national child protection policy (U.S. Advisory Board, 1991). The response by federal authorities has been disappointing, however. Congressional staff initially were enthusiastic about the possibility of broad-scale reform to protect children and even delayed reauthorisation of the Child Abuse Prevention and Treatment Act (CAPTA) in order to attempt to achieve it. Unfortunately, though, the ultimate form of the reauthorisation (Child Abuse Programs, 1992) included only new findings (rather than a binding policy), did not touch the Public Health Service, the Cooperative Extension Service, or other agencies potentially important in the new strategy, and failed to provide significant changes to remedy the serious problems in the National Center on Child Abuse and Neglect. Despite early indications of interest, Congress also did not address the need for substantial development of the Department of Justice's role in child protection when it reauthorised the Juvenile Justice and Delinquency Prevention Act (Juvenile Justice, 1992).

The Bush Administration showed even less concern for the dire conditions facing hundreds of thousands of American children. It showed no interest at all in the CAPTA reauthorisation, until amendments were proposed to increase the independence of the U.S. Advisory Board on Child Abuse and Neglect, after which a bevy of high-ranking officials in the Administration for Children and Families appeared on Capitol Hill to lobby key congressional staff. Similarly, the

Board's initial declaration of a national emergency would not have reached the public if Board members and staff had not themselves called the media, because Department of Health and Human Services public affairs staff did not distribute a press release until hours before the press conference at which the report was to be released--ostensibly because they could not decide whose stationery to use. Such action, even if not intended as outright obstruction, certainly trivialised the gravity of the threats to the safety of many American children.

At the same time, though, the Board's reports have resonated among professionals in the field, and some significant action has been undertaken, especially within the voluntary sector. Most notably, the National Committee for the Prevention of Child Abuse launched Healthy Families America (funded by the Ronald McDonald Foundation). The principal focus of that initiative is an attempt to build universal infant home visiting programmes for the purpose of prevention of child maltreatment--the U.S. Advisory Board's top-priority recommendation in its 1991 report. Healthy Families America now has stimulated progress toward that goal in the majority of states.

More generally, there appears to be a new Zeitgeist in children's services, with widespread recognition that traditional human services are poorly matched to the needs of many children and families in the various public service systems (Melton & Hargrove, in press). Services for children and families work best when they follow the Jericho Principle--tearing down metaphorical walls of diagnosis and discipline and going outside physical walls of office buildings and institutions to blend services into "natural" settings where children and families live, study, work, and play (Melton, 1989b; Melton & Pagliocca, 1992). Accordingly, collaboration, coordination and integration of services have become buzzwords in child welfare (Borthel, 1992), child mental health (Stroul & Friedman, 1986), education (Knitzer, 1990), juvenile justice (Barton et al., 1991), and other domains of child and family services (Soler & Schauffer, 1990). Many state legislatures have enacted statutes designed to promote such service system reform, especially through demonstration programmes (Smith, 1991).

The ideological changes that have occurred among planners and providers of child and family services and the initiatives that have resulted thus open the door to development of a service system that is responsive to the needs of changing families. Unfortunately, though, there are few signs that policy makers and programme administrators are ready to carry such insights and demonstration programmes to their logical conclusion through broad-based reform of financing, agency structure, and professional education. The opportunity now is present for a service system that is conceptually based and consistent with values ostensibly fundamental to public policy (e.g., family integrity), but formidable obstacles stand in the way of accomplishment of more than modest reform.

CHILDREN IN A TIME OF CHANGE: THE BIG PICTURE

THE CONVENTION AND THE WORLD SUMMIT

My sense that we are at a global moment of truth, at least in regard to children and families, has been heightened by my experiences in countries where a sense of crisis is not necessarily widespread.   I have been involved in several conferences and consultations designed to facilitate implementation of the Convention on the Rights of the Child in Australia and Western Europe.

Certainly the most remarkable events have been the unprecedented speed and universality of ratification of the Convention on the Rights of the Child (1989), coupled with the World Summit for Children, the largest assembly of heads of state in history. The leaders gathered at the U.N. promised to meet 27 goals in the 1990s--most of them related to improvement of child health and education.

The symbolic significance of these events is obvious. The import of the Convention and the Summit Declaration goes far beyond the international analogue to a baby-kissing ritual, though. First, even the symbolism is momentous. Only 25 years have passed since the personhood of children was formally recognised in the United States (In re Gault, 1967), probably the most rights-conscious nation in the world. The disgraceful failure of President Bush to sign the Convention and submit it to the Senate for ratification (a failure that President Clinton has yet to indicate that he plans to rectify) suggests that the United States may have been left behind in leadership on such matters; the United States remains virtually the only Western democracy on the list of non-signatories.   Nonetheless, the *Gault* case offers a useful benchmark for consideration of how far the world has come. The Convention must seem truly revolutionary in societies where recognition of civil and political rights for adults is recent and the cultural norm for adult behaviour toward children traditionally has been at least hierarchical and sometimes openly authoritarian.

In that regard, one of the most interesting aspects of implementation of the Convention (1989), has been the response in much of Latin America. All Latin American governments are parties to the Convention, and several have sponsored nationwide celebrations or education efforts (eg Ecuadoran Supreme Electoral Court, 1990).

When the Convention eventually is ratified by the United States, it is conceivable that it will transform children's law in this country. Although few provisions of the Convention are in direct conflict with American law (Cohen & Davidson, 1990; American Bar Association, 1993), full implementation of the Convention would be momentous. American courts are used to interpreting "constitutional" language of the sort that permeates the Convention, and they could lead in giving meaning to the Convention in developed countries. Thus ratification of the Convention may foster more careful consideration of the ingredients necessary for protection of dignity of children (Melton, 1991b)--not just, for example, the rudiments of due process rights available to adult defendants but also those procedures that are necessary for juvenile respondents to *feel* that they are treated "in a manner consistent with the promotion of the child's dignity and worth," so that they build "respect for the human rights and fundamental freedoms of others" and that they "assume a constructive role in society" (Convention, 1989, art. 40, § 1; cf. Melton, 1989a).

Moreover, even if the Convention is regarded as not fully self-executing (see ABA, 1993), the ratification of a treaty recognising social and economic rights-- an unprecedented act in American history--would offer legislatures guideposts that could have spectacular effects on children and families. Imagine the significance of a "right of every child to a standard of living adequate for the child's physical, mental, spiritual, moral, and social development" (Convention, 1989, art. 27, § 1)--to "enjoyment of the highest attainable standard of health care" (art. 24, § 1), to education aimed at "the development of the child's personality, talents and mental and physical abilities to their fullest potential" (art. 29, § 1(a)), to cultural activities that permit full participation of children (art. 31).

Second, the adoption of the Convention and the Summit Declaration occurred with fortuitous timing, because the global situation has changed in ways that make their implementation feasible. For example, the international community had made a promise in the late 1970s, when only 10% of children in developing countries were immunised to reach a goal of 80% immunisation by 1990--with the result that the lives of almost nine thousand children are saved each day (Grant, 1992). This extraordinary achievement--like those that the World Summit conferees hope to accomplish during the present decade, was made possible by political change that recognised the importance of *people* and the diminution of world tension so that money could begin to be diverted from military spending to investment in the survival of children.

Third, the Convention has increased the structures available to monitor children's rights and increase attention to children's interests in policy making--a development that could ultimately have ramifications far beyond those germane to the Convention itself. The Convention requires states parties to submit periodic reports to a committee of experts (Convention, 1989, arts. 43-44), and it provides roles for nongovernmental organisations and specialised international agencies (e.g., UNICEF) in monitoring and technical assistance in implementation of the Convention (Convention, 1989, art. 45). Perhaps more important, the authority and coherence of the Convention are such that it has provided a framework to inform discussions of child and family even in non-ratifying countries (Newman-Black, 1991).

Although the euphoria of child advocates around the world in the adoption of the Convention is justified, caveats also are warranted. As I have already noted, some of the most powerful nations in the world either have not ratified the

Convention or have failed thus far to apply it broadly. Perhaps an even more telling fact is that the timing of the World Summit for Children was such that it provided an opportunity for Western leaders to strategise about their response to the Iraqi invasion of Kuwait, and it was that side activity that grabbed the headlines more than the extraordinary gathering to consider the needs of the world's children.

Ultimately, the gap between the Convention's promise and its fulfilment is clear when one realises that it should affect not just *what* the state does in its relations with children but *how* it is done. For example, the Convention guarantees not just that rehabilitative services are provided to maltreated children but that they "take place in an environment which fosters the health, self-respect and dignity of the child" (Convention, 1989, art. 39).

Unfortunately, my experience in international conferences and consultation to national governments is that the import of the Convention as a constitution for the world's children often is being missed, as both politicians and advocates focus on compliance in a narrow sense. As is too often the case in international human rights law, the Convention is being used to some extent as authority for condemning the evil nation (typically, evil Third World country) of the month club (e.g., Brazil, for its scandalous treatment of street children). Although atrocities merit the condemnation of the international community, no Convention was necessary for that purpose. Rather, the utility of the Convention lies primarily in the guidance that it could give developed democracies in development of policies consistent with the dignity of their youngest citizens. For the most part, the Convention's meaning is missed if its principles--many of which are purposefully incremental and expansive--are thought to be susceptible to a dichotomous choice (comply/not comply). In short, the Convention *could* be the source of a new concern with the personhood of children and a worldwide revolution in children's policy--or it could be mere platitudes that serve only as another basis for condemnation of the outcasts from the global community.

CHILDREN AND WAR

Another marker signifying that the world is at a turning point in its treatment of children has been the evolution in the status of children in war zones. When the Summit Declaration was adopted, the conferees urged "earliest possible ratification and implementation" of the Convention on the Rights of the Child, and they noted one particular domain in which the spirit of the Convention should be applied with singular zeal: special protection for children in time of war.

Although the foundation for such an agenda in the Convention actually is rather weak (Convention, 1989, art. 38, § 4), the need is undeniable. A by-product of the development of military technology has been that armed conflict now typically is literally "war on children." In World War I, 5% of the casualties were civilians; the proportion in contemporary conflicts is 80% - most of them women and children (Grant, 1992). As was vividly portrayed in the weeks following the Iraq war (Raundalen, undated) and as has been echoed in the current wars in former Yugoslavia (Battiata, 1992), the indirect effects of war on children also can be devastating, as the supply of food and medicine diminishes and schools and clinics close.

The one bright spot in this gruesome reality is that the customary law of armed conflict does appear to be moving in the direction recommended by the Summit conferees. With little fanfare, a new rule appears to be developing to require periodic cessation of hostilities so that humanitarian relief can be given to children:

> In El Salvador, civil war has been suspended on three separate days every year for the last seven years so that children can be immunised. In Lebanon, "days of tranquillity" allowed children to be vaccinated even at the height of the troubles. In Sudan, both sides eventually agreed to "corridors of peace," through which essential supplies could reach millions of civilians, mostly women and children, trapped in the war zone. Similar agreements have since been negotiated in Angola and Ethiopia. In Iraq, essential medical supplies were delivered even at the height of the Gulf conflict (Grant, 1992, p. 26).

Most recently, days of tranquillity were declared in Bosnia (Pfaff, 1992; Reid, 1992).

Although the risk to children in war zones from infectious diseases is sometimes even greater than the risk that they experience from war itself, there admittedly is something perverse about a brief cessation of conflict to vaccinate children who are at risk of being maimed or killed when the shooting resumes. Nonetheless, one should not minimise the message that the world community, even in its darkest hours and its most troubled places, is beginning to recognise its responsibility to minimise the wrongs inflicted on children when adults resort to armed conflict.

At the same time, one should not lose sight of the fact that children have been the victims of special atrocities in some of the conflicts in recent years. Lawrence Aber (see DeAngelis, 1992), James Garbarino (Garbarino, Dubrow, & Kostelny, 1991, 1992; Garbarino, Kostelny, & Dubrow, 1992), Magne Raundalen (Dodge & Raundalen, 1987, 1991), and their colleagues have painted haunting verbal pictures of recent warfare against children, sometimes reaching extraordinary levels of barbarism.

One also should not forget the warfare that has erupted in some of our own neighbourhoods. Garbarino et al.'s summary is both insightful and disturbing:

> What horrifies us most about the war in Chicago is the suspicion that rules for the combatants are deteriorating. The killing becomes steadily more casual, and more bestial. Drugs drive and accelerate this process. A mother who was nearly shot cries out, "They don't care about nothin' anymore. They shoot their own mother if she got in their way." When the war is beyond caring, the slide to barbarism is often precipitous (Garbarino, Kostelny, & Dubrow, 1991, pp. 158-159).

One quarter of youth on the Southside of Chicago reported having witnessed a murder by the time they were 17, and all children in some public housing projects in that city had first-hand knowledge of shootings by the time that they were 5 (Garbarino, 1992a). About 40% of children in some New Orleans neighbourhoods report having seen dead bodies on the streets. Nearly half of fifth- and sixth-graders in Southeast Washington have witnessed severe violence (Youngstrom, 1992). More teenage boys in the United States die of gunshot wounds than all natural causes combined--a rate of victimisation that increased dramatically in the second half of the 1980s (National Commission on Children, 1991).

The impression that we are at a crossroads is again present. On the one hand, at least small steps are being taken to limit children's victimisation in war. On the other hand, both means and venues for violence against children seem to be increasing in disturbing ways with bloody and numbing consequences.

CHILDREN AND POVERTY

Because of its pervasiveness and its power in impeding the healthy development of children (DaVanzo, 1992), the biggest threat to a new world order that is inclusive of children probably is poverty. The adage that "the rich get richer, and the poor get poorer" has had special meaning for children in recent years.

In the United States, income for people in the bottom two quintiles declined in the last decade, income for those in the top 20% increased by almost 30%, and income for the top 1% increased by almost 75%. Moreover, bad times have been sustained for many people at the bottom of the economic ladder. The proportion of poor people who moved out of poverty declined by nearly 40% in the 1980s (Garbarino, 1992a).

On a global scale, average incomes in the majority of developing countries dropped substantially during the 1980s--by 10% in Latin America and 25% in Africa (Grant, 1992). Poor countries with a heavy debt have shown even more marked decline. The result is that health, education, and nutrition of children in much of sub-Saharan Africa has regressed to colonial levels (UNICEF, 1992).

At home, poverty rates among young families have doubled since the 1970s; real incomes for families headed by a worker under age 25 declined by one-fourth between 1973 and 1989 (National Commission, 1991). One in four infants and toddlers - one in five of all children - lives in poverty. One in 11 children under age 6 lives in a desperately poor family--one whose income is only half of the poverty level (Korbin, 1992).

The dire position of children in our society is unprecedented. Not only are children the poorest age group, but the outlook for them is the bleakest (Moynihan, 1987). Upward mobility is no longer the expectation for America's youth. In part as a result, adolescence is being effectively extended as young adults remain in their parents' home for increasingly longer periods of time (Office of Educational Research, 1988).

The high level of poverty among American children has costs beyond the immediate suffering resulting a low standard of living. As the National Commission on Children (1991) recognised, the effects reverberate:

> Most poor children in America are at double jeopardy. They experience the most health problems but live in the least healthful environments and have the least access to medical care. They are at the highest risk of academic failure, but often attend the worst schools. Their families experience the most stress but have the fewest social support. (p. 29)

Again, we are at a crossroads. In the light of the new world political situation, substantial reduction of child poverty now is affordable. Such an achievement would require, however, that we reverse the transfers of income that have occurred since 1980 from poor to rich in the United States and from South to North in the world as a whole. The risk of exacerbating those perverse trends remains.

Failure to act positively will result in more and more neighbourhoods that are essentially uninhabitable in safety. Poverty is becoming increasingly concentrated, with spiralling negative momentum in the quality of life in some neighbourhoods. For example, 21% of poor people in Cleveland lived in a high-poverty area in 1970; by 1988, the proportion had more than doubled to 50% (Coulton & Pandey, 1992). As those residents who can gather any assets by their exceptional competence or sheer luck continue to leave declining inner-city neighbourhoods, rural communities, and small towns, the result will be an increasingly desperate class of "have-nots" who not only lack the funds necessary for a decent standard of living but who also live in social poverty, as the pool of young, reasonably successful families who themselves can serve as resources declines and as fear of each other rises among those who remain. The result for children will be increased insecurity and widened gaps between actual and potential development.

CHILDREN IN RECENT HISTORY

Although some of these events and trends are tied to the political events that I discussed earlier, it is important not to lose sight of the fact that they follow *three decades* of extraordinary change in the lives of children and families throughout the developed world. In the last quarter century in the United States, the divorce rate nearly quadrupled, fertility fell by half, the number of children living with one parent almost tripled, and the rate of children being born outside wedlock also quadrupled (Popenoe, 1989).

These dramatic changes in family life are "evident, in varying degrees, in every industrialised Western country, which suggests that their source lies not in particular political or economic systems but in the broad cultural shift that has accompanied industrialisation and urbanisation" (Popenoe, 1990, p. 43). In keeping with that conclusion, family law - a domain noted historically for its emphasis on conflicts of law across jurisdictions - now is equally remarkable for its consistency across not only American states but also nations with quite different cultures and political histories (Melton, 1988). As the economic relationship between men and women has changed, so too have the law and reality of family life. Family relationships now are grounded less in social obligation and economic need and more in the need for personal fulfilment, with the result that familial duties increasingly give way to other concerns.

At the same time that the family has changed dramatically, so too have the communities that serve as its context. In combination, the changes in the family and the community have strikingly decreased the availability of informal support for children within them. We are moving further and further from an environment for child development that includes:

> a relatively large family that does a lot things together, has many routines and traditions, and provides a great deal of quality contact time between adults and children; regular contact with relatives, active friendships in a supportive neighbourhood, and contact with the adult world of work; little concern on the part of children that their parents will break up; and the coming together of all these ingredients in the development of a rich family subculture that has lasting meaning and strongly promulgates family values such as cooperation and sharing (Popenoe, 1989, p. 4).

The instability of social support for children and families can be inferred from the striking statistics on the mobility of American families. Almost one in five Americans - one in four young children and one in three young adults - lives in a home different from the residence occupied a year earlier (Bureau of the Census, 1990, table 25). Isolation and mobility are associated with the same variables that correlate positively with number of stressors that people experience (Melton, in press) - variables that also are related to child maltreatment (Garbarino &

Kostelny, 1992; Garbarino & Sherman, 1980). Thus the families that are most in need of support are those who are least likely to have it easily available.

The everyday significance of these social changes was strikingly demonstrated in surveys that a research team that I headed conducted in a prosperous city in South Carolina (see, e.g., Melton, 1992a). Interviews of representative samples of parents in various neighbourhoods have shown stunning class differences in their families' perceived safety and quality of life. Many inner-city parents could think of nothing good about their neighbourhood, and the problems that they identified were predominantly ones of basic safety (i.e., drugs, crime, and traffic). On the other hand, many suburban parents could think of no problems for families in their neighbourhood, and they had relatively few concerns about their children's safety.

At the same time, though, there were disturbing and somewhat surprising similarities across poor and affluent neighbourhoods. When asked to whom they go for help when their children have problems, parents in general - unlike respondents thirty years ago (Gurin et al., 1960) - generally did not mention day-to-day sources of help like neighbours, relatives, clergy, and family physicians. About two in five parents in both inner-city and suburban neighbourhoods could think of no agency, organisation, or group that was making their community a better place for families to live. The majority (regardless of social class) regarded parents in their neighbourhoods as lacking involvement with other families' children. The majority also could think of no instance in which they themselves had done anything to help a child in the community.

These findings give a graphic picture of the crisis. The service system has not caught up with the social change that has transformed neighbourhoods and families. The National Commission on Children (1991) has noted the consequences of such social change for children and families:

> Traditionally, communities have been a source of informal support, of neighbourly assistance. For many Americans, however, the sense of belonging to a community has been displaced by isolation and anonymity. Greater mobility in our society means that fewer relatives and friends are nearby to lend a hand. Social isolation cuts across class lines, but it is often most pronounced in poor neighbourhoods, where everyone is under stress and few adults or children have the personal stamina or resources to support others. Rebuilding a sense of community and reinvigorating informal systems of support for families and children should be a primary goal of social policies. Extended families, including grandparents, aunts, uncles, and cousins, represent a rich source of support. We believe the supports that improve life most are those which convey the message that one is not alone, that someone else cares and will be there to help in times of trouble and need. (pp. 70-71, footnotes omitted)

There also is evidence, though, for a new familism (Whitehead, 1992). In the last five years, the annual surveys of high school seniors and college freshmen across the United States have shown substantial upturns among both males and females in the proportion who label raising a family as a very important objective (Glenn, 1992; Popenoe, 1992). Such data are paralleled by research showing increasing respect for children, as manifest, for example, by increasing disapproval of corporal punishment of children and of berating them (National Committee for Prevention of Child Abuse, 1992; Newell, 1992). The challenge is to find new ways to make use of such concern to reduce the isolation that many children and families now experience.

BUILDING A PLACE FOR CHILDREN: TOWARD A RENAISSANCE FOR FAMILIES

Much of the recent innovation in child and family policy and services in the United States can be traced to the work of the late Nicholas Hobbs (1966, 1982), a president of the American Psychological Association. In a book written at the request of Elliot Richardson, then secretary of health, education, and welfare, and Edward Zigler, then director of the Office of Child Development, Professor Hobbs (1975) issued a prescient call for "a renaissance of family life." He passionately asserted what has become all too clear today: "the nation cannot neglect children, nurture them in violence, and expect them to grow up to be good citizens, concerned with the well-being of their fellow man" (Hobbs, 1975, p. 15).

I can improve little on Professor Hobbs's succinct statement of the task before us:

> There is urgent need for a quickened national conscience and a new national policy with this as a goal: to nurture well all of our children, in body, mind and spirit, that we as a people may grow in wisdom, strength, and humane concerns....

The nation's best bet for reducing the prevalence and severity of mental retardation, emotional disturbance, antisocial behaviour, and a host of other personally limiting and socially costly disabilities is to mount developmental and preventive programmes from childhood on and to maintain them dependably as long as need is present. The best bet for breaking the cycle of poverty and perpetuated social incompetence is to strengthen the family, to work with parents and potential parents and with their children from the earliest years in a sustained press for healthy emotional, intellectual, and social development (Hobbs, 1975, pp. 14-15).

I would add that the best bet for strengthening families and fostering an attitude of respect for children as individuals is to build or rebuild neighbourhoods. In the post-industrial age, we need to build new connections among people, caring communities in which adult watch out not only for their own but also their neighbours' families. I would add further that the need now is for a quickened *global* conscience that *humanity* may grow in wisdom, strength, and humane concerns.

In this context and taking advantage of the opportunities presented by the nearly worldwide acceptance of the Convention on the Rights of the Child, we must be sure to provide means to hear the voices of children. We need to recognise the contributions that children and youth often can make to their communities. Such a combination of participation and representation is likely to do much to promote children's dignity. We must listen, and we must act so that crisis becomes opportunity.

We are indeed at a time of global liberation - a liberation of the human spirit enabled by the growth of a world-wide marketplace of ideas, a development itself facilitated by the expansion of communications and information technology. That liberation and the resulting deceleration of the arms race permit redistribution of wealth--perhaps more precisely, reinvestment of wealth--to free children both at home and abroad from the bondage of poverty, disease, and ignorance. The exchange of ideas also reveals the logical and moral force of the concept of personhood and opens the door to the *experience* of being treated as a person worthy of respect - discussions and experiences that enable a greater understanding of the meaning of personhood for children.

We have the *possibility* for a renaissance - an age of enlightenment premised on respect for the dignity of children as persons. Taking children seriously is likely to facilitate their intellectual, social, and moral development, and meeting their basic material needs will provide the foundation for healthy maturation. Building a new sense of community will promote a network to support families and to offer connections among people necessary for a strong social fabric.

With momentous opportunities, though, comes momentous peril. We have the *risk* of an age of anomie--of rising isolation, anger, and desperation among the disadvantaged people of the world.

The risk that children's interests will be neglected is the risk that we will miss the opportunity for a new world order in which respect for humanity is the linchpin of political life. The development of the Third World (and, one might add, Eastern Europe) rests in large part on the choices that it makes about children's rights (see Bross, 1991). Economic development is inseparably linked to education leading to personal achievement, which in turn is affected by sense of self-respect--a trait that is based in early experiences with autonomy and privacy (Tremper & Kelly, 1987). Democracy further rests on a sense of equality - respect for others - derived from consistent nurturance leading to a basic trust in people (Bross, 1991).

Thus fulfilment of children's rights is likely to have important future effects. It is often argued that healthy socialisation is important for adult productivity. Surely that point is worth consideration. The more important point in regard to survival of an open society, though, may be that early experience in being treated as a person worthy of respect builds a sense of personal significance (of others as well as oneself). Involvement in the community and tolerance of diversity then are perceived as worthwhile and even morally obligatory.

When a society recognises the personhood of its smallest and most vulnerable members and not only protects them but does so in a manner that promotes their dignity, it sets a tone conducive to promotion of democratic ideals. When such conditions are not present, the message is clear that raw power is more important than either reason or caring. In much of the world, either scenario is a plausible reality for the future. We have the choice of a *community* that is a healthy place for children to grow or - as vividly illustrated by events in former Yugoslavia, Los Angeles, and elsewhere - ever more pronounced and violent *division* into enclaves separated by race, ethnicity, class, and age.

Is there a place for children in the new world order? I hope so.

REFERENCES

Bar-on, M. (1991, February/March). The Israeli-Palestinian conflict: A Zionist perspective. *New Outlook*, p. 33.

Barthel, J. (1992). *For children's sake: The promise of family preservation*. New York: Edna McConnell Clark Foundation.

Barton, W. H., Streit, S. M., & Schwartz, I. M. (1991). *A blueprint for youth corrections*. Ann Arbor, MI: University of Michigan, Center for Study of Youth Policy.

Battiata, M. (1992). The littlest victims in the land of the living dead. *Washington Post National Weekly Edition*, November 30-December 6, 1992, 16.

Bronfenbrenner, U. (1961). The mirror image in Soviet-American relations: A social psychologist's report. *Journal of Social Issues, 17*, 3, 45-56.

Bross, D. C. (1991). The rights of children and national development: Five models. *Child Abuse and Neglect, 15, Supp. 1*, 89-97.

Bureau of the Census (1990). *Statistical abstract of the United States, 110th edition*. Washington, D.C.: U.S. Government Printing Office.

Castle-Kanerova, M. (1992). Social policy in Czechoslovakia. In B. Deacon, et al. (Eds.), *The new Eastern Europe: Social policy past, present and future*. London: Sage.

Child Abuse Programs, Adoption Opportunities, and Family Violence Amendments Act of 1992, Pub. L. 102-295, 106 Stat. 187, *reauthorizing* Child Abuse Prevention and Treatment Act, 42 U.S.C. §§ 5101 et seq.

Cohen, C. P., & Davidson, H. A. (Eds.). (1990). *Children's rights in America: U.N. Convention on the rights of the child compared with United States law*. Washington, D.C.: American Bar Association, Center on Children and the Law; New York: Defense for Children International-U.S.A.

Cohn-Donnelly, A., & Mitchel, L. (1992). Memorandum to Healthy Families America partners, December, 4, 1992.

Coulton, C. J., & Pandey, S. (1992). Geographic concentration of poverty and risk to children in urban neighborhoods. *American Behavioral Scientist, 35*, 238-257.

Daro, D., Downs, B., Keeton, K., McCurdy, K., Beard, S., & Keaton, A. (1991). *World perspectives on child abuse: An international resource book*. Chicago: National Committee for Prevention of Child Abuse.

DaVanzo, J. (1992). Families, children, poverty, policy. In J. B. Steinberg, D. W. Lyon, & M. E. Vaiana (Eds.), *Urban America: Policy choices for Los Angeles and the Nation* (pp. 83-104). New York: Rand Corporation.

David, H. P., Dytrych, Z., Matejcek, Z., & Schuller, V. (Eds.) (1988). *Born unwanted: Developmental effects of denied abortion*. New York: Springer; Prague: Avicenum.

Deacon, B. (1992). East European welfare: Past, present and future, in comparative context. In B. Deacon, et al., (Eds.), *The new Eastern Europe: Social policy past, present and future*. London: Sage.

Deacon, B. (1992). The future of social policy. In B. Deacon, et al., (Eds.), *The new Eastern Europe: Social policy past, present and future*. London: Sage.

Deacon, B., & Vidinova, A. (1992). Social policy in Bulgaria. In B. Deacon, et al., (Eds.), *The new Eastern Europe: Social policy past, present and future*. London: Sage.

DeAngelis, T. (1992). Children's reactions to war are examined. *APA Monitor, 23*, 9, 34.

DeAngelis, T. (1991). Living with violence: Children suffer, cope. *APA Monitor, 22*, 1, 26-27.

Detrick, S. (Ed.). (1992). *The United Nations Convention on the Rights of the Child: A Guide to the "Travaux Préparatoires"*. Dordrehct, the Netherlands: Martinus Nijhoff.

Dodge, C. P., & Raundalen, M. (Eds.). (1991). *Reaching children in war*. Uppsala, Sweden: Scandinavian Institute of African Studies.

Dunovsky, J. (1991, November). *Concepts and approaches to the syndrome of abused and   neglected child in Czechoslovakia within the context in Europe*. Paper presented at a People to People seminar in Prague.

Dunovsky, J. (1990, July). *The children in Eastern Europe*. Paper presented at a meeting at the UNICEF International Child Development Centre, Florence, Italy.

Ecuadoran Supreme Electoral Court, UNICEF, and the Central Bank of Ecuador (1990). *Los derechos de los niños y la democracia [The rights of the child and democracy]*. Quito: Author.

Flekkøy, M. G. (1991). *A voice for children: Speaking out as their Ombudsman*. London: Jessica Kingsley.

Freeman, M., & Veerman, P. (Eds.). (1992). *Ideologies of children's rights*. Dordrect, the Netherlands: Matinus Nijhoff.

Garbarino, J. (1992b). The meaning of poverty in the world of children. *American Behavioral Scientist, 35*, 220-237.

Garbarino, J. (1992a). Coping with the consequences of community violence. *Protecting Children, 9*, 1, 3-5, 18.

Garbarino, J., Dubrow, N., Kostelny, K., & Pardo, C. (1992). *Children in danger: Coping with the consequences of community violence*. San Francisco: Jossey-Bass.

Garbarino, J., & Kostelny, K. (1992). Child maltreatment as a community problem. *Child Abuse and Neglect, 16*, 455-464.

Garbarino, J., Kostelny, K., & Dubrow, N. (1991). *No place to be a child: Growing up in a war zone*. Lexington, MA: Lexington Books.

Garbarino, J., Dubrow, N., & Kostelny, K. (1991). What children can tell us about living in danger. *American Psychologist, 46*, 376-383.

Garbarino, J., & Sherman, D. (1980). High-risk neighborhoods and high-risk f families: The human ecology of child maltreatment. *Child Development, 51*, 188-198.

Glenn, N. (1992). What the numbers say. *Family Affairs,*

Grant, J. P. (1992). *The state of the world's children.* Published for UNICEF. New York: Oxford University Press.

Greenbaum, C. W. (1991, February/March). Child in distress: Psychology and politics. *New Outlook,* pp. 39-40.

Gullestad, M. (1991). The transformation of the Norwegian notion of everyday life. *American Ethnologist, 18*, 480-499.

Gullestad, M. (1984). *Kitchen table society: A case study of the family life and friendships of young working class mothers in urban Norway.* Oslo: Universitetsforlaget; Irvington-on-Hudson, NY: Columbia University Press.

Gurin, G., Veroff, J., & Feld, S. (1960). *Americans view their mental health: A nationwide survey.* New York: Basic Books.

Havel, V. (1992). *Summer meditation on politics, morality and civility in a time of transition.* Boston: Faber & Faber.

Henggeler, S. W., & Borduin, C. M. (1990). *Family therapy and beyond: A multisystemic approach to treating the behavior problems of children and adolescents.* Pacific Grove, CA: Brooks-Cole.

Himes, J. R., Kessler, S., & Landers, C. (1991). *Children in institutions in Central and Eastern Europe.* Florence, Italy: UNICEF International Child Development Centre.

Hobbs, N. (1982). *The troubled and troubling child.* San Francisco: Jossey-Bass.

Hobbs, N. (1975). *The futures of children: Categories, labels, and their consequences.* San Francisco: Jossey-Bass.

Juvenile Justice and Delinquency Prevention Amendments of 1992, Pub. L. 102-586, 106 Stat. 4982.

Kalish, S. (1993). Life expectancy falling, morbidity rising in former U.S.S.R. *Populations Today, 21*, 1-2.

Knitzer, J., Steinberg, Z., & Fleisch, B. (1990). *At the Schoolhouse door: An examination of programmes and policies for children with behavioral and emotional problems*. New York: Banks Street College of Education.

Korbin, J. (1992). Introduction: Child poverty in the United States. *American Behavioral Scientist, 35*, 213-219.

Korbin, J. (Ed.). (1992). Symposium, the impact of poverty. *American Behavioral Scientist, 35*, 213-339.

Kordacki, J. (1991). Blindness to child abuse in Poland. *Child Abuse and Neglect, 15*, 616-617.

Kovaik, J. (1991, November 14). Remarks to the Citizen Ambassador Delegation, Prague.

Krugman, R. D. (1990). Returning to Europe: Expanding horizons. *Child Abuse and Neglect, 14*, 299.

Landes, E., & Posner, R. A. (1987). *The economic structure of tort law*. Cambridge, MA: Harvard University Press.

Lewis, H. (1991, February/March). Enforced ignorance is also a wound. *New Outlook*, p. 41.

Lief, L., et al. (1991, October 14). Juggling guns and butter. *U.S. News and World Report*, p. 49.

Manning, N. (1992). Social policy in the Soviet Union and its successors. In B. Deacon, et al. (Eds.), *The new Eastern Europe: Social policy past, present and future*. London: Sage.

Melton, G. B. (1988). The significance of law in the everyday lives of children and families. *Georgia Law Review, 22*, 851-895.

Melton, G. B. (1989a). Taking *Gault* seriously: Toward a new juvenile court. *Nebraska Law Review, 68*, 146-181.

Melton, G. B. (1989b). The Jericho principle: Lessons from epidemiological research. In L. W. Abramczyk (Ed.), *Social work education for working with seriously emotionally disturbed children and adolescents* (pp. 12-25). Columbia, SC: National Association of Deans and Directors of Schools of Social Work.

Melton, G. B. (Ed.). (1991a). *Journal of the Citizen Ambassador Program Child Welfare Delegation to Poland, the Soviet Union, and Czechoslovakia*, available from People to People, Spokane, WA.

Melton, G. B. (1991b). Lessons from Norway: The children's ombudsman as a voice for children. *Case Western Reserve Journal of International Law, 23*, 197-254.

Melton, G. B. (1991c). Socialization in the global community: Respect for the dignity of children. *American Psychologist, 46*, 66-71.

Melton, G. B. (1992a). It's time for neighborhood research and action. *Child Abuse and Neglect, 16*, 909-913.

Melton, G. B. (1992b). The law is a good thing (Psychology is, too). *Law and Human Behavior, 16*, 381-398.

Melton, G. B. (1993). Anarchy ain't so great. *Law and Human Behaviour, 17*, 259-260.

Melton, G. B. (in press). Children, families, and the courts in the twenty-first century. *Southern California Law Review*.

Melton, G. B., & Hargrove, D. S. (in press). *Planning mental health services for children and youth*. New York: Guilford Press.

Melton, G. B., & Pagliocca, P. (1992). Treatment in the juvenile justice system: Directions for policy and practice. In J. J. Cocozza (Ed.), *Responding to the mental health needs of youth in the juvenile justice system*. Seattle: National Coalition for the Mentally Ill in the Criminal Justice System.

Mezentseva, E., & Rimachevskaya, N. (1990). The Soviet country. Profile: Health of the U.S.S.R. population in the '70s and '80s. *Social Science and Medicine, 31*, 867-877.

Millard, F. (1992). Social policy in Poland. In B. Deacon, et al. (Eds.), *The new Eastern Europe: Social policy past, present and future*. London: Sage. Deacon, B. (1992). East European welfare: Past, present and future, in comparative context. In B. Deacon, et al., (Eds.), *The new Eastern Europe: Social policy past, present and future*. London: Sage.

Ministry of Health, Czech Republic. (1990). *Reform of health care in the Czech Republic: Draft of a new system of health care*. Prague: Author. (Second version Oct. 28, 1990)

Ministry of Health and Social Welfare, Czech Republic. (1991). *People to People mission to Poland: Background papers*. Prague: Author.

Mission to the Czech and Slovak Federal Republic. (1991). *The health sector: Issues and Priorities*. Prague: Author.

Moynihan, D. P. (1987). *Family and nation*. San Diego: Harcourt Brace Jovanovich.

National Commission on Children. (1991). *Beyond rhetoric: A new American agenda for children and families*. Washington, D.C.: U.S. Government Printing Office.

National Commission on Foster Care. (1991). *A blueprint for fostering infants, children, and youths in the 1990s*. Child Welfare League of America, National Foster Parent Association, Washington, D.C.

Nelson, B, (1984). *Making an issue of child abuse: Political agenda setting for social problems*. Chicago: University of Chicago Press.

Newell, P. (1992). Testimony before the U.S. Advisory Board in Child Abuse and Neglect at a hearing in Chicago on International Perspectives on a New Strategy for Child Protection in the United States, August 29, 1992.

Newman-Black, M. (1991). Introduction. In M. Newman-Black & P. Light (Eds.), *The convention: Child rights and UNICEF experience at the country level*. Florence, Italy: UNICEF International Child Development Centre.

Office of Educational Research and Improvement (1988). *Youth indicators 1988: Trends in the well-being of American youth*. Washington, D.C.: Office of Educational Research and Improvement.

Passell, P. (1992, March 15). A peace dividend for Israel. *New York Times, § 3*, p. 5.

Pfaff, W. (1992, September 26-27). Helping in Bosnia: Aid workers get on with a dangerous job. *International Herald Tribune*, p. 4.

Popenoe, D. (1992, Winter/Spring). [Untitled Comment]. *Family Affairs*, p. 11.

Popenoe, D. (1990). Family decline in America. In Blankenhorn, D., Bayme, S., & Elshtain, J. B. (1990), *Rebuilding the nest: A new commitment to the American family*. Milwaukee: Family Service America.

Popenoe, D. (1989, Summer/Fall). The family transformed. *Family Affairs*, pp. 1-2.

Price Cohen, C., & Davidson, H. A. (Eds.) (1993). *Children's rights in America: U.N. Convention on the Rights of the Child Compared with United States Law*. Washington, D.C.: American Bar Association Center on Children and the Law; New York: Defense for Children International.

Raundalen, M. (undated). *The long term impact of the Gulf War on the children of Iraq*. Available from Research for Children, Bergen, Norway.

Reid, R. (1992). *Children's rights: Radical remedies for critical needs*. Paper presented at the Conference for Justice for Children, University of Glasgow, Scotland.

Smith, S. L. (1991, June). *Family preservation services: State legislative initiatives*. Denver: National Conference of State Legislatures.

Soler, M. I., & Schauffer, C. (1990). Fighting framentation: Coordination of services for children and families. *Nebraska Law Review, 69*, 278-297.

Statistisk Sentralbyrå (1992). *Children in Norway: Mini-facts*. Oslo: Author.

Stroul, B. A., & Friedman, R. M. (1986). *A system of care for severely emotionally disturbed children and youth*. Washington, D.C.: Georgetown University Child Development Center, CASSP Technical Assistance Center.

Szalai, J., & Orosz, E. (1992). Social policy in Hungary. In B. Deacon, et al. (Eds.), *The new Eastern Europe: Social policy past, present and future*. London: Sage.

Thompson, R. A. (1992). *Social support and the prevention of child maltreatment*. Paper presented for the U.S. Advisory Board on Child Abuse and Neglect.

Tiang-Yau Liu, J. (1992). *The health of America's children 1992: Maternal and child health data book*. Washington, DC: Children's Defense Fund.

Tremper, C. R., & Kelly, M. P. (1987). The mental health rationale for policies fostering minors' autonomy. *International Journal of Law and Psychiatry, 10*, 111-127.

UNICEF International Child Development Centre (1992). Economic decline and child survival: Evidence from Africa in the 1980s. *Innocenti Update*, 1

58

U.S. Advisory Board on Child Abuse and Neglect. (1991). *Creating caring communities: Blueprint for an effective federal policy on child abuse and neglect*. Washington, D.C.: U.S. Government Printing Office.

U.S. Advisory Board on Child Abuse and Neglect. (1990). *Responding to a national emergency: Critical first steps toward a national strategy on child abuse and neglect*. Washington, D.C.: U.S. Government Printing Office.

Veerman, P. (1991, February/March). Helping Israeli and Palestinian youngsters. *New Outlook*, pp. 43-44.

Veerman, P., & Samaan, G. (1992). A review of DCI-Israel's legal aid project. *Israel Children's Rights Monitor, 3*, 35.

White, R. K. (1977). Misperceptions of the Arab-Israeli conflict. *Journal of Social Issues, 33*, 1, 190-221.

Whitehead, B. D. (1992, Winter/Spring). A new familism? *Family Affairs*, p. 1.

Youngstrom, N. (1992). Inner-city youth tell of life in a "war zone". *APA Monitor, 23*, 2, 36.

CHAPTER 3

JUSTICE FOR CHILDREN THROUGH THE UN CONVENTION

Thomas Hammarberg

Two years ago leading statesmen from all over the world met in New York to discuss children. More than 70 heads of Government or State came, as well as some 90 other senior officials. Never before had so many world leaders gathered for a meeting.

The original idea for this World Summit met with little response, but when the preparation at last was under way more and more leaders announced their willingness to attend. The bandwagon was moving and few wanted to be seen as insensitive to the fate of children.

This was no surprise. It is a well known phenomenon that politicians make gestures to appear child-friendly. Of course some of them are genuinely concerned, perhaps influenced by their own family background. But there are also those who use children for their own propaganda purposes.

This was probably one factor which made the United Nations Convention of the Rights of the Child possible. When the process of drafting this convention had started, few government representatives took the trouble to oppose the various proposals to protect and support children.

Perhaps they thought that the whole thing was harmless; they might have been influenced by the fact that children's issues on the international scene often have been seen as a matter of charity - feeling pity and being kind to small ones.

In fact, one view has been that problems related to children are noncontroversial. It was assumed that everyone agreed, so these issues were seen as nonpartisan and above politics. However, the truth is that the conditions for children in many countries - and internationally - have been put outside the political agenda. This depoliticisation has been to the detriment of children. When it has come to the crunch other interests have been given priority at the cost of those related to the rights of the child.

CHARITY OR RIGHTS?

This has been a concern of the children's rights movement ever since it first emerged. During the years after the First World War, soon after some concrete progress was made in the struggle for the equality of women,, the idea that children, too, had rights took root for the first time in Europe. Typically, it was the women who had taken part in the fight for their own equal status who carried the banner of the rights of the child.

One of these was Eglantyne Jebb from Great Britain who launched a campaign of solidarity with children who had suffered during and immediately after the war in Europe - including those who happened to live on the "other" side. She was prosecuted for having exhibited pictures in public of undernourished children. As the children were undressed her action was branded as "obscene".

The publicity about this court case gave the new movement an extra momentum. Save the Children was founded in London in May 1919 and some months later in Sweden. A five-point declaration on the rights of the child was drafted. In 1924 this text was adopted by the League of Nations. The rights of the child had become a recognised concept.

Eglantyne Jebb and the other drafters of this first declaration grasped the essentially political character of the problem. She said that "it is children who pay the highest price for our short-sighted economic policy, our political blunders, our wars". Her point was that children were often victims of politics. They needed rights for their protection which could only be established through political changes.

There is a clear difference between such an approach and charity. The very idea of children's rights is that society has an obligation to satisfy the fundamental needs of children. Charity is not as far-reaching. Though often based on a genuine compassion for little ones, that approach tends to stop at kindness. It does not speak of rights and treats children as objects rather than allowing them to become subjects.

It is on this very point the UN Convention on the Rights of the Child is so definitely important. One of its main messages is that children's issues are political - and should be put high on the political agenda. Article 4 of the convention states:

> "States Parties shall undertake all appropriate legislative, administrative, and other measures for the implementation of the rights recognised in the present Convention. With regard to economic, social and cultural rights, State Parties shall undertake such measures to the maximum extent of their available resources and, where needed, within the framework of international cooperation."

In plain words: give priority to children! This is the same thought as the one expressed in slogans like "Children first!" or "First call for children!".

FROM DECLARATION TO TREATY

The road from the first declaration in 1924 to the convention in 1989 was not straightforward. When discussions started after the Second World War about international norms for the protection of human rights, some people noted that children had little protection and even less influence. An attempt was made to develop the 1924 declaration and a longer text of a similar nature was adopted in 1959.

But neither of these declarations were binding on the governments of the world; they were significant statements of principle, but no more. Therefore, an idea emerged about drafting a treaty between governments on the rights of the child. In the late seventies the United Nations agreed in principle on this proposal.

The decision to embark on the project to draft a special convention for children was not obvious. One objection was that children already were covered by existing codes of human rights, eg the two UN human rights covenants. Specific norms protecting children in particular were included in several of the rights treaties. Some people even argued that it would be to the disadvantage of children if their rights were singled out in a special convention; special treatment can sometimes lead to discrimination.

However, it became evident that the existing codes of human rights were inadequate to meet the special needs of children. Reality itself was the strongest argument in favour of a convention. There were reports on grave injustices suffered by children - infant mortality, deficient health care for children and unacceptably limited possibilities for basic education. There were also shocking accounts of how children were exploited as prostitutes or in harmful jobs, about children in prisons or in difficult circumstances as refugees or war victims.

Another reason for a convention was that the thinking on the rights of the child had developed substantially since the 1959 declaration was adopted. There was now a greater awareness of the psychological needs of children. Also, more people had woken up to the fact that the interests of children were not necessarily identical to those of their guardians; it was clear that many children were badly treated within the framework of the family.

The process started within the UN Commission of Human Rights and a special working group under that body. Ten years later, in November 1989, the text was ready for adoption. One feature had been particularly important during the drafting work: nongovernmental organisations had been allowed to take part and had managed to put forward many proposals based on practical experience of working directly with children.

The World Summit helped promote the Convention and now more than 120 countries have ratified. This is remarkable. No other international human rights treaty has had so many ratifications in such a short time. Even after 25 years of existence the International Covenant on Civil and Political Rights and its equivalent on Economic, Social and Cultural Rights have not gained as much support. In fact, countries which have not acceded to any other international human rights document are among those which have ratified the one for children.

Why is this? Maybe for the reason I mentioned earlier: children are seen as a popular cause. Perhaps also, some governments really have decided to give priority to children and to respect their rights. Others have probably not fully understood the obligations which follow from the ratification. This makes it all the more important to make clear what the Convention actually says.

A NEW ATTITUDE - THE PRINCIPLES OF THE CONVENTION

The philosophy behind the Convention is that children, too, are equals; as human beings they have the same value as grown-ups. The right to play underlines that childhood has a value in itself; these years are not merely a training period for adult life. The idea that children have equal value may sound like a truism, but it is, in fact, a radical thought - not at all respected today.

However, children - especially when very young - are of course vulnerable and need special support to be able to enjoy their rights in full.

The combination of these two thoughts is the drama of the Convention. How do we grant children equal value and at the same time grant them the necessary protection? One conclusion is the principle of "the best interests of the child". It is most clearly formulated in article 3,1:

> "In all actions concerning children, whether undertaken by public or private social welfare institutions, courts of law, administrative authorities or legislative bodies, the best interests of the child shall be a primary consideration."

There is an element of "children first" in this article. When decisions are taken which affect children, their interests should be seen as important. The interests of the state or the parents should not be regarded as the all-important consideration.

It follows that we should also listen to the voices of children themselves. Article 12.1 deals with this aspect:

States Parties shall assure to the child who is capable of forming his or her own views the right to express those views freely in all matters affecting the child, the views of the child being given due weight in accordance with the age and maturity of the child."

Other articles stipulate that the child has rights to freedom of expression, freedom of thought, freedom of conscience and even freedom of assembly. The formulations on these points are not very specific but the message is still clear: the opinions of children should be given respect. If this spirit was implemented it would indeed change the reality in most countries.

These principles are combined in the text with the demand that children, precisely because they are children, must be given special protection. Otherwise their rights to life, health and development would be endangered. But, again, the need for this protection is no excuse for reducing children to mere objects.

Another fundamental principle of the Convention is that all children should enjoy their rights and no child should suffer discrimination. The obligation to provide equality of opportunities among children is expressed in article 2, the first paragraph of which reads:

"States Parties shall respect and ensure the rights set forth in the present Convention to each child within their jurisdiction without discrimination of any kind, irrespective of the child's or his or her parent's or legal guardian's race, colour, sex, language, religion, political or other opinion, national, ethnic or social origin, property, disability, birth or other status."

The principles that children have equal value as human beings, that the best interests of the child should be a primary consideration, that due weight should be given to the child's opinion and that each child has rights are all of great importance. Together they form nothing less than a new attitude towards children. They give an ethical and ideological dimension to the Convention.

What caused the horrible misery in the Romanian institutions for disabled children was not lack of resources, it was an authoritarian attitude which reduced certain children to unwanted creatures, a sort of social waste. That was an extreme example, but in fact many violations of children's rights are based on such values contradicting the very spirit of the Convention.

I have emphasised the visions and ideas of the convention because I believe these will be at least as important as the concrete elements. A true implementation of the Convention must respect the principles therein.

SPECIFIC ARTICLES CONCERNED WITH BASIC NEEDS

The substantive articles are meant to cover all kinds of human rights: economic, social, cultural, as well as civil and political rights. The division between these categories of rights, which often has plagued the United Nations discussion on human rights generally, is not reflected in this convention. It has an integrated approach. The various rights are not ranked in order of priority; instead they interact with one another to form part of the same entity.

The very first article of the Convention defines which individuals are covered by the norms. A child is defined as every human below the age of 18 years, unless majority is attained earlier according to the law of the country. Obviously, this wording is the result of a compromise. Majority is attained at 18 in a number of countries; but it is reached earlier in some countries and later in one or two other countries. To reach an international agreement on the age of majority was not considered possible. However, the mentioning of 18 still forms some kind of a benchmark.

The most important aspect of the definition is of course that it makes clear that the Convention covers not only smaller children, but also those who have reached their teens. The substantive articles could be grouped into three categories: the right to have one's basic needs met; the right to protection against exploitation and discrimination and the right to express one's opinions and have them respected.

It is only natural that the Convention lays stress on the basic needs, like the rights to health care and education. One key obligation for governments is to "ensure to the maximum extent possible the survival and development of the child" (article 6, 2).

The emphasis on health is strong. Governments are required to take measures to reduce infant and child mortality, develop primary health care through the use of readily available technology and provide adequate nutritious food and clean drinking water. They are also under an obligation to give information and education about child health and nutrition, the advantages of breast-feeding, hygiene and environmental sanitation and the prevention of accidents (article 24).

The right to education is another aspect on which emphasis is laid. Primary education shall be compulsory, free and available to all (article 28).

RIGHT TO PROTECTION

The articles on security and protection are both general and targeted. They deal with the kind of protection that all children require, but also with the need for special efforts on behalf of children in especially difficult circumstances.

The Convention raises the question of corporal punishment. Governments are under an obligation to take measures "against all forms of physical or mental violence, injury or abuse, neglect or negligent treatment, maltreatment or exploitation" (article 19.1). The article refers specifically to the family environment or other child care situations. Another article stipulates that school discipline must be upheld in a manner "consistent with the child's dignity" (article 28.2).

The Convention states that no child shall be subjected to torture or other cruel, inhuman or degrading treatment or punishment. Neither capital punishment nor life imprisonment without the possibility of release shall be imposed for offences committed by persons below the age of 18. This age limit shall apply also in countries where majority is attained at an earlier age (article 37).

There is no absolute ban on the imprisonment of minors; but detention of young offenders should only be used as a last resort and for the shortest possible period of time. Every child deprived of liberty must be treated with humanity and in a manner that takes into account the needs of persons of their age. Imprisoned children are to be separated from adults if it is considered to be in the best interests of the child (article 37).

Children shall be protected from the illicit use of narcotic drugs and governments shall prevent the use of children in the production and trafficking of such substances (article 33).

The Convention specifically refers to the right of protection from all forms of sexual exploitation, such as prostitution and other unlawful activity. Governments must also ensure that children are not used for pornographic purposes (article 34). Governments are also obliged to prevent the abduction, sale of or traffic in children (article 34). Children have to be protected from economic exploitation and from performing any work that is likely to be harmful to their health or development (article 32.1).

The article dealing with children in armed conflicts was debated more than any other article during the process of drafting the text. The most controversial aspect concerns child soldiers. Voluntary organisations and several governments proposed that the age limit for recruiting soldiers, particularly for combat duties, should be set at 18. This faced opposition from, above all, the representatives from the United States. The outcome was that the limit was set as low as 15 years but recruitment into armed forces from those aged between 15 and 18 should give priority to those who are oldest (article 38).

The question of refugee children is given particular attention. One article reiterates rights enjoyed by refugees under the relevant international instruments. The Convention does not request that all children seeking refugee status automatically be granted asylum, but they shall be entitled to receive "appropriate protection and humanitarian assistance" in the enjoyment of the rights they have according to international law (article 22).

Oppression of minorities is also covered in the Convention. Children belonging to ethnic, religious or linguistic minorities or who are of indigenous origin shall have the right to enjoy their own culture, to profess and practice his or her own religion, or to use his or her own language (article 30).

The question of adoption is regulated in a quite precise way. The best interests of the child are to be the paramount consideration. Intercountry adoption is recognised as an alternative means of a child's care, if the child cannot be placed in a foster or adopive family in its country of origin (article 21).

One group of children specifically mentioned are disabled children. These children are entitled to enjoy a full and decent life and governments shall promote the active participation of these children in society. The support given to them should be free of charge. The disabled child should have access to education and training, health care and rehabilitation services, preparation for employment and recreation opportunities. The aim is to contribute to the fullest possible social integration (article 23).

The Convention demands that measures are taken against female circumcision ("traditional practices prejudicial to the health of children"), a violation that young girls are subjected to in certain countries. The fact that unanimity was reached over this issue was a major step forward in the international work for the rights of girls (article 24.3).

The issue of abortion arose during the drafting process. The only result was a reference in the preamble of the Convention to the point "that the child due to his or her physical and mental immaturity needs special protection, both before and after birth".

Some anti-abortionists have interpreted this as a legal support for their position. However, the issue of abortion is not mentioned at all in the operational parts of the Convention, despite the fact that such proposals were made in the discussions. The drafters, in fact, agreed not to include a norm against abortion. Thus, the Convention does not commit itself one way or the other on abortion.

THE CHILD, GUARDIANS AND THE STATE

The authorities are under obligation to take measures to protect children from physical and mental abuse by their parents or other legal guardians. The Convention accepts that an intervention might be necessary to separate a child from his or her family environment precisely in order to prevent various forms of ill-treatment or neglect (article 19).

Thereby it is made clear that the child's interests and those of the legal guardians do not necessarily coincide. This is a significant aspect of the Convention; we know from experience that some of the worst abuses perpetrated against children do take place behind family doors.

That is not to say that the Convention is hostile towards the family. On the contrary, in several places it underlines the importance of the child being able to grow up in a secure family environment. In fact, the Convention states early on that the family should be afforded necessary support and assistance. It goes on to declare that "the child, for the full and harmonious development of his or her personality, should grow up in a family environment, in an atmosphere of happiness, love and understanding". These passages in the preamble are reflected in the operational parts of the Convention.

Parental rights are indeed recognised. States are requested to respect the responsibilities, rights and duties of parents or legal guardians to provide "appropriate direction" in the child's exercise of his or her rights. The term "appropriate" signals a qualification; the direction is to be provided "in a manner consistent with the evolving capacities of the child". Again, the idea is that the child be given more influence with greater age and maturity.

When it is stressed that the legal guardians have "the primary responsibility for the upbringing and development of the child", there is also a qualification: the best interests of the child (article 18.1).

The same thought is included in the article stating that a child separated from one or both of his or her parents, shall have the right to maintain personal relations and a direct contact with both parents. Again, the principle of the child's best interests may override this (article 9, 3).

The article dealing with freedom of thought, conscience and religion gives parents the right to provide direction to their children regarding their outlook on life. The provision is directed against governments that are intolerant in this respect. But, again, there is a restriction on parents; the direction shall be exercised "in a manner consistent with the evolving capacities of the child" (article 14).

The triangular relationship between children, legal guardians and the authorities is thus treated by the Convention in a balanced manner. Children are seen as separate individuals with rights of their own, while at the same time recognising the importance of parents or other legal guardians for the child's development.

Thus, the state is expected to support the families. Only when the family becomes a threat to the child, should society intervene, with the protection of the child as the primary objective. In that event, the intervention shall be made with respect for the legal rights of the parties concerned, but a primary consideration is the best interests of the child.

The Convention as such is not formally binding on individuals. For example, parents are not bound by it. It is the government of each country that is respons- ible for ensuring that the norms laid down in the Convention are adhered to in actual practice; for instance, by enacting laws governing parental rights and duties in respect of children in accordance with the Convention.

THE REALITY

So far I have described the content of the Convention, but will it make a difference? Will its principles and concrete norms be respected?

Of course reality will not change at a stroke. The problems are enormous on the global scale. Ten million children die each year as a result of curable diseases and malnourishment. More than one hundred million children are to-day deprived of primary education. Almost as many are exploited in harmful jobs. Hundreds of thousands of girls and boys are abused in prostitution. A growing number of children have been infected by HIV.

Many children are victimised by war - as soldiers or as part of a terrorised civilian population. Ten million children are refugees inside or outside their own country. Millions of disabled children are forgotten or discriminated against. Children are suffering physical violence even in their own homes in most parts of the world.

THE COMMITTEE

There is no international court which can sanction these or other violations against the convention, but since February 1991 an elected expert committee has been monitoring the implementation in the countries which have ratified.

According to the Convention itself, the ten experts in the Committee on the Rights of the Child were elected in their individual capacities, rather than as voices of the ten countries of which they are citizens.

Those elected in the first round come from the Philippines, Russia (then the Soviet Union), Sweden, Portugal, Egypt, Burkina Faso, Zimbabwe, Barbados, Peru and Brazil. The Brazilian member has since resigned and left us with a vacancy. The members have various backgrounds; law, medicine, politics, church work, journalism, development aid work, social science and social work. Six of those elected are women, four men.

Future elections to the Committee will take place every two years and on each such occasion half of the Committee will be elected for a four year period. The elections will be held at a special meeting in the UN headquarters in New York and each party to the Convention will have a vote.

The procedures laid down in the Convention call for State Parties to report to the Committee on implementation for the first time within two years after ratification. The first reports were due in September 1992. For the one and a half years thereafter more than a hundred governments are to submit their reports which puts a heavy burden indeed on the Committee.

It decided during its first meeting that each report should be responded to within one year after submission. This has raised the problem of its meetings: how often and how long can it meet? The original intention among governments, though never clearly spelled out, was that it would meet once a year for two or three weeks.

This is clearly not sufficient. The Committee estimates that on average each country report will require at least six hours at the final stage of scrutinising by the full Committee, when the government will be invited to send a representative. Before that there is a need for preparations. The intention is, furthermore to invite comments from nongovernmental organisations and UN bodies and specialised agencies, like UNICEF and ILO.

The Committee therefore requested to be allowed to meet twice a year for two to three weeks and that a sub-committee could meet for another week in advance of each full Committee meeting.

At the end of its deliberation on a country's report, the Committee will make concluding observations. The hope is that this public statement will promote discussion in the reporting country and form the basis for improvements until the next report is due after another five years. It is an important aspect of this process that it enhances public discussion of children's issues. The reports themselves should be made widely available to the public within the country concerned. The Committee, in turn, is to report every two years to the United Nations General Assembly.

The procedures for monitoring the rights of the child by the Committee will be different from the usual models in the field of human rights. The thrust is not finger-pointing but rather constructive and aid-oriented. The aim is that the Committee - together with the reporting government and any aid agencies involved - should attempt to define the problems and discuss what remedies are necessary.

The Convention recognises the problem of limited resources in poor countries and says that governments should undertake appropriate measures in accordance with their available resources. This might turn out to be an unfortunate escape clause, but it is significant that the same article points to the possibility of international assistance. This will probably be helpful for the work of the Committee in relation to developing countries. No other international human rights instrument makes such a clear linkage between reports on violations and development aid. In fact, it is said in the text of the Convention that the Committee shall transmit requests for aid to the specialised UN agencies, UNICEF and other competent bodies, along with observations and suggestions.

The problem, however, remains that it will not be easy for the Committee to evaluate the implementation of some of the provisions in the Convention - for instance, the one on "child survival" - as the concrete obligations are not specified in the text of the Convention. In particular, evaluating economic and social rights of a collective nature will require a creative approach by the Committee. The main point is whether governments will demonstrate a genuine intention, a political will, to provide such rights. Will they take steps to implement the Convention "to the maximum extent of their available resources"?

ENCOURAGING DISCUSSION

Although the Convention is part of international law, it is what the lawyers usually call a "soft law". One objective is to develop moral standards regarding the treatment of children. The sanctions include unfavourable publicity and pressure, phenomena that do not easily lend themselves to definition.

Some previous UN human rights conventions have been significant and have had an actual effect on reality; others have more or less been forgotten. The risk that the Convention of the Rights of the Child will fall into oblivion is minute give the amount of attention it has already attracted. Many voluntary organisations, such as Save the Children, have decided to use it as a platform for their work.

The true significance of the Convention will be determined by the degree to which it becomes more generally known and to what extent it forms the basis for political and other work concerning children. For that reason it is important that its contents are spread to the public at large, not least to the youngest generations.

In this connection, the Convention itself lays down an important requirement. Governments are under an obligation to make its provisions and principles widely known (article 42). Voluntary organisations will be able to play an important supplementary role in this context. The same goes for the mass media.

It is particularly important that people whose work involves responsibility for children - at kindergartens, schools, within the health service and so on - are provided with information about the Convention as well as with opportunities to study it further. The education system should inform children of their rights.

The Committee has emphasised that the process should be designed to encourage a debate over the plight of children in each country. The reports from governments ought not be the sole concern of an individual government official. The statements should be seen as a stimulus for a thorough investigation of the position of children in society.

The various articles in the Convention may be seen as an agenda for such debates. Even countries that formally fulfil the obligations laid down by the convention will find ideas for further discussion.

Such a discussion would be further stimulated if the government takes account of the views of voluntary organisations in connection with the drafting of the reports. National children's rights committees with representatives of governments and nongovernmental organisations have already been formed in some countries.

ACHIEVEMENTS ALREADY

It would of course be premature to try to assess the real impact of this convention. At the same time, it should be stressed that the very fact that it has been drafted, adopted, ratified and has come into force is an achievement in itself.

- The Convention has given us a **universal definition** of the very concept of the rights of the child. It is a definition which cuts through all social systems as well as all cultural and religious views. This is a significant step. It will no longer be possible to defend oppression of children on the grounds that it is a custom within that particular culture.

- Conceptual progress has been made in that the Convention gives children and teenagers the **status of human beings with full rights**. Children are to be respected as individuals in their own right: they are not the belongings of someone else. The Convention must thus be regarded as a step forward in the struggle for the equality of children.

- The very use of the term "rights" challenges **the charitable approach** which for so long has dominated the way in which children's issues have been addressed - with a regrettable depoliticisation of these issues.

- It is to be hoped that this in turn will make it easier to show how children are affected by the major crises of our day: the poverty gap, the wars and the conflict and the environmental pollution. That will, hopefully, contribute to a **political awakening** that will be absolutely necessary if we are to solve these critical matters of survival.

- The Convention will in all probability result in **increased political attention** being given to children and young people. The Convention can from now on serve as an "agenda" for the discussion of the actual circumstances of children. The process required by the Convention, whereby reports have to be submitted on a regular basis and discussions held, should lead to regular examination in every country of issues relating to children and young people.

- The link established by the Convention between the reports by the states and discussions about development aid may become a dynamic element in aid policies.

- The Convention could also serve as a **starting-point for further standard-setting** within the field of children's and young people's rights. An area where follow-up work will soon have to be undertaken is connected to the protection of children in armed conflicts. The Convention is obviously not a final product. Instead, it should be seen as the first and important milestone.

CHAPTER 4

NATIONAL POLICIES ON CHILDREN'S RIGHTS AND INTERNATIONAL NORMS

Savitri Goonesekere

International standards on Children's rights have been developed in the post war decades on the basis that a strategy of rights can be integrated into policy planning so as to achieve the goal of justice for children. When we speak today of fundamental rights, human rights and children's rights, we thus assume a common value base which provides the conceptual foundation for those rights. We also assume that the realisation of those rights will help to achieve a uniform kind of justice or equity. Yet there are some who would argue that all these concepts are relative and must necessarily be interpreted differently according to the social and economic or cultural context of a particular nation. It has sometimes been said that human rights in international law reflect exclusively Eurocentric and even male oriented norms. A lawyer who is familiar with the differences between the Scottish legal tradition derived from Roman Law, and the English Common Law tradition can adopt a purist's approach and say that there are fundamental differences in the concepts of equity and justice developed in these distinct legal traditions.

When differences are emphasised and recognised as a reflection of different societal needs, it is easy to conclude that there must necessarily be varying concepts of rights, and different models of justice, in countries that belong to the world community. As long as people including some activists for children, accept the premise that rights are relative and that justice takes its tone from the socio-economic and cultural environment, they will feel constrained to recognise that the standards they set for their children are different to those they set for other's children. This legitimacy for different standards creates and fosters in my view a kind of insensitivity to the problems faced by children placed by accident of birth in a cultural or socio-economic context that they themselves are powerless to alter. A small child from a low income family who is deprived by adults of his or her childhood is easily perceived as a child enjoying the right to participate in the important task of ensuring family survival. The circumcision or early marriage of girls is as easily described as a positive social practice that may be relevant and meaningful in ensuring early social conditioning, which in turn fosters family and community solidarity in place of a Eurocentric and ruthless ideology of self fulfilment. Inevitably the standards of rights justice and equity set for low income children or children belonging to minority ethnic or religious groups and particularly children in the developing countries become specific to their own context. The ambivalence in regard to standards prevents the creation of a solid consensus on the ultimate goals that we wish to achieve in advocating a strategy for children rights.

In contrast to this relativist position, I would like to argue that we live in a global situation where it is meaningful to speak in terms of universal norms and standards that are relevant for all children. We must recognise that channels of media and communication as well as political and economic forces have broken national frontiers and exposed people all over the world to new pressures that impact on some aspects of their lives. If these global events and trends alter the quality of life of people, how justifiable is it to perceive cultural and religious traditions, or socio-economic situations as unchanging and unchanged?

The pursuit of structural adjustment policies and market economies for instance has introduced new values of consumerism that undermine traditional attitudes towards family and community solidarity in developing countries. Low income parents in Pakistan, India, Bangladesh and Sri Lanka are persuaded to trade their children in marriage to rich bridegrooms from the Gulf States, Japan or Europe. The girl travels overseas and may be lost in a brothel or become a virtual slave in another family. Traditional marriage practices thus become an easy path to international trafficking and prostitution. Low income children in South and South East Asia may in the past have been treated as part of the family unit of production and worked with his or her family as feudal tenants in the fields, in a household or in a colonial and post colonial plantation economy. The deprivation of childhood that occurred in that situation can hardly be compared with the anguish a child faces today when he/she becomes the family earner as a non-paid domestic servant or a worker in a sweat shop or industrial work place. The consumer ethos, international migration and the economics of industrial production also foster the inclination to exploit the labour of young workers. They are docile, cheap, and particularly useful for performing certain tasks. Migration of women workers to the Gulf States in search of employment for instance has increased the incidence of child labour in domestic service in Sri Lanka. Small boys from the subcontinent as well as Sri Lanka are taken illegally across borders to be trained as camel riders or jockeys for winter sports in the Gulf States. Countries which do not employ their own children in this risky and dangerous activity think nothing of employing low income Asian children for the same purpose. Thus child care is for our children; child work is the destiny of `others' children.

The legal and social legitimacy for the practice of using children in domestic service, in agriculture or industrial production fosters new forms of exploitation and confronts children with new risks. Child abduction in Pakistan is linked to the presence of labour camps in certain areas which provide child labour for industrial enterprises and construction sites. When low income families are deeply affected by a rising cost of living and inadequate resources for survival, traditional values concerning family supports for weaker members are rejected in favour of sending children out to earn their own keep or contribute to family survival.

In this situation, the child is placed at risk because of a conflict of interest between adults and children. Similarly the value placed on child care and nurturing is undermined by the focus on an adult family member's right to perceive the child as an economic resource or to use the child to care for siblings so that the adult can take employment outside the home. The concept of equitable treatment for children then comes into conflict with adult rights and the goal of achieving access to employment for adult men and women. Policies on women in development that do not give adequate priority to child care can undermine the care and nurturing children receive according to traditional values in many communities in Asia and Africa.

It also seems facile to ignore the impact of modern governmental power and the international trade in dangerous weapons on the lives of children all over the world. The State and paramilitary groups today, more than ever before, are equipped to use and abuse power and authority. When street children are picked up as vagrants, placed in detention or even eliminated the State is using its role as protector of society against children who are themselves not responsible for their economic situation and the pressures this creates. All children are exposed more that ever before to new levels of violence in political conflicts, within the family, and the community, because of the violence of a gun culture. There is surely universality in the situation of violence, faced by children all over the world. The risks faced by these children are no different to risks faced by those early citizens whose conflicts with the State produced what Scottish law, continental European and Anglo-American law now recognise as legal protections based on due process or natural justice. The peasant in South Asia who today lies on a mat in the dark in anguished fear of the authorities or paramilitary groups needs the protection of due process as much as any person who has the right to that protection, as a result of a modern or Eurocentric legal system which recognises the concept of human rights.

Do not concepts of cultural relativism also impact negatively on children who must today face the pressure of conflicting values in plural societies? It seems unrealistic to refer to homogeneity in cultural values in any context when customary and cultural traditions have themselves been exposed to the impact of colonialism, a new economic order, and new forces of highly political religious fundamentalism which negate the humanism and tolerance of the great world religions.

Socio-legal research in both Asia and Africa has shown how British colonial laws and policies impacted on both the content and the application of customary laws and practices. The concept that the father is the natural guardian of children, which is today considered a fundamental premise of the law in many countries of

76

Asia and Africa, did not in fact originate in the customary or religious laws of
these regions. It was received from an English Common law or Roman legal
tradition and identified by the rulers with what they perceived as existing norms.
Customary values of family support and inheritance on the other hand have been
undermined through a long period of colonial rule and in post-independence
trends. The concepts of family and parental rights therefore function in a context
where changes over the years and a new economic order do not provide support
for assumption of familial responsibility for children or the elderly.

More recently consumerism and a wave of religious fundamentalism in South and
South East Asia has undermined the traditional rights and status of women,
placing girl children at risk of exploitation within families and communities.
Women activists in Pakistan, for instance, claim that new policies derived from a
new perception of religious norms have undermined the recognised position of
women in Islam. At a time when these women are seeking to see the
compatibility between religious norms and international standards, an ideology
that stresses the importance of cultural and religious values even when they
contradict international standards undermines the legitimacy of efforts to make
that linkage. Children themselves are placed at risk by families that adhere to
ethnic or religious values that conflict with values recognised by majority
communities. While adults resist change on the argument that majoritism must
be resisted and cultural pluralism should be recognised, children's lives are
affected by the recognition of a different scale of values. For instance Sri Lankan
courts have recently recognised that a Muslim parent's obligation to educate a
minor son extends to a shorter period of time than in the case of other
communities, and that a child adopted legally by Muslim parents has a different
legal status from other adopted children [1]

These problems of legal pluralism today are not confined to the countries of Asia
and Africa which have experienced colonialism. The phenomenon of migration
into the United Kingdom, Europe, the United States and other countries has now
placed minority children in a situation where they are exposed to a risk of
conflicting norms and values. If cultural and religious rights are to receive
official recognition even when they undermine State norms, what is the vision of
justice or rights that is to be projected for the country? If some people have rights
that are not enjoyed by others, will not this undermine the very values of rights,
justice and equity the State wishes to endorse for the majority? If parents can
deny the education rights of a child from one community because they feel that
he/she should stay at home, and the State respects that parental decision, what
does this do to the State policy on compulsory education? The Supreme Court of

---

[1] Ummul Marzoona v. Samad (1977) 79 N.L.R. 209; Ghouse v. Ghouse (1988) 1
Sri L.R. 25

the United States faced this problem in the Yoder Case.[2] The majority held with the parents in a situation where the child identified with the parents' views and the difference of opinion between the parents and the authorities was in regard to the type of education the child was to receive. However if the child is not consulted, or expresses a different view from his/her parents, can the concept of double standards undermine the general State policies on education?

If the State does not take a stand on values, it leaves the child in a limbo where conflict of interest between the child and the family may be resolved through violence. This has happened in cases reported recently by the press in both the United States and England. In two cases, parents used violence against children who did not conform with the norms of their community. That violence can be prosecuted on the basis of the Criminal law of the country, but if cultural pluralism receives priority, a cultural defence may be pleaded in mitigation of sentence. Can the cultural context be considered in interpreting the concept of reason for the defence of provocation? Once the concept of cultural relativism in standards is recognised, the conduct of the parent in a minority group will inevitably have to be addressed by a different standard - with dangerous consequences for the child.

These are strong reasons for committing ourselves to the idea that the norm of justice for children throughout the world must be a universal norm. This in fact is the philosophy reflected in the U.N. Convention on the Rights of the Child. For the first time, an important instrument has placed before the world community a set of standards that represents a uniform rights strategy, that in its realisation puts forward a common concept or vision of justice. We know that recognition of rights for children presupposes that responsibilities will be imposed on adults as well as children. The concept of justice envisaged in the Convention is not confined to realisation of rights.

The framework of Rights developed by the Convention has received a great deal of publicity since it was adopted in 1989. Much has been written and spoken, and there is some general awareness that the Convention recognises rights of survival and development, protection and participation. It is the realisation of these rights that is expected to create a just and equitable national and international ethos for children. The link between these rights is a vital aspect of the universal standards for children, set by the Convention. In the past, a country might content itself to setting a goal of child survival and growth, focusing on reducing infant mortality and fostering early child development through health care and immunisation. The Convention however requires parallel developments to realise the other rights of children. States Parties to the Convention must recognise that a child has a right to survival because he/she has a right to grow and develop, be

---

2 Wisconsin v. Yoder 406 U.S. 205

protected from exploitation or deprivation of childhood in the family and the community, and also participate, as he/she matures, in important decisions that affect a child's life. Thus, States Parties must commit themselves to the goal of reducing infant mortality, because they are also committed to preventing child marriage, excluding children from the workplace and bringing them into the school system. Participation rights involve respect for the child's right to be protected from adult exploitation and to choose not to be thrust into the workplace or early marriage because of adult needs. If the concept of justice in the Convention is to be realised, countries must no longer perceive low income children merely as persons placed in difficult circumstances but as children whose governments have failed to fulfil their responsibilities under the Convention. For the Convention, in my view, has set standards for both ratifying and non-ratifying States Parties.

It is true that it is ratification of the Convention that creates obligations under international law, and gives the Committee on the Rights of the Child the legal status to monitor national performance. However, ratification does not, in most countries of the world, particularly in Asia and Africa, automatically make these international standards part of national law. The local legislature and the courts have to act in such a way as to bring these standards into the national system. Law reform within a country will be necessary. If the Convention is ratified, a government has an obligation to initiate legal and other reforms. It should also publicise the Convention, as well as its own regular report of performance to the monitoring committee. This will undoubtedly strengthen the hand of activists and concerned organisations to monitor performance and violations, and help them to lobby for creative change at the national level.

Nevertheless, absence of ratification cannot hamper these efforts to initiate national reforms, because an international consensus has grown in regard to the validity of the standards set by the Convention. The large number of ratifications, the World Summit for Children and the focus on developing national plans of action in conformity with the World Plan of Action and Goals for Children, encourage monitoring treatment of children in all countries even if a country has not become a party to the Convention by ratification.

If the Convention has created an international concept of justice, it could nonetheless be argued that problems connected with administration of justice for children may require that we have different models of administration of justice. Again I would like to suggest the opposite - that it is possible to develop similar models that can be replicated in different countries of the world. Realisation of Convention standards within developed and developing countries will often require a State to address some issues which are very similar, despite the dramatic differences in the socio-economic and cultural contexts.

Let us take the crucial aspect of State and family responsibility for children. The Convention has put forward a new value in suggesting that legislators, administrators, and the courts - the three official components of government - as well as the family and private and public welfare organisations - give priority to the best interests of the child. The Convention has also recognised the concept of `parental responsibility' in place of parental rights that has already been developed in the Children Act (1989) which introduced reforms in the English law on children. It is parental responsibility that creates a sphere of parental authority as well as a child's rights in his/her family and the community. In place of the concept of non-intervention of family privacy however, the Convention has put forward the idea of State responsibility to support parents in fulfilling their responsibility to protect and realise the best interests of the child. The crucial concept of justice for children puts forward the idea that children have a right to resources from the community and the State has a responsibility to ensure that adequate resources are provided to families to care for children. A low income family child thus has the same rights as other children to resources, and it is the responsibility of the State to ensure that this equity is realised through its own efforts and with private sector participation. There can be no double standards in this regard, because the concept of realising justice for children through a strategy of rights demands that countries develop or work towards a model of equitable resource allocation. Fiscal and development policies must be judged by this international standard. UNICEF's annual survey on the state of the world's children thus provides hard evidence that can be used to ask why resources for health and education receive low priority.

The problem of pluralism in cultural and religious traditions and the role of uniform legal values and development policies in plural societies, was once a problem peculiar to colonised nations. This is now a global issue, with the increase in international migration, refugee problems and the growth of a sense of ethnic and minority community identities. The growth and development of common social and legal norms between diverse communities in Asia and Africa shows how cross-fertilisation of ideas has taken place so as to forge a common set of values. Similarly the impact of colonialism in Asia and Africa resulted in the spread of common norms through a process by which colonial norms displaced traditional norms in the area of private law, and new norms of constitutional practice and governance replaced traditional norms. In areas such as marriage and child law, colonial legal values administered in colonial courts acquired a dominant status and led to changes in traditional law. Similarly citizens opted out of traditional systems by choosing to govern family relations according to colonial codes that put forward a different scale of values. This in turn strengthened uniformity and undermined pluralism in the law. The Criminal law and post-independence Constitutions also put forward values derived from Anglo-American jurisprudence, with regard to due process and protection from violence in the family or community. These prevented cultural values being used to justify violence, in particular against women and children. British colonial laws on the practice of Sathi or wife immolation, infanticide, exorcism rituals and infringements on personal liberty, are examples that indicate how State compulsory policies were imposed without giving citizens the choice of opting out of these uniform legal regimes.

The United Nations Convention on the Rights of the Child has provisions which require respect for cultural pluralism, and freedom of thought and conscience. These concepts must be accommodated within the concept of justice for children that recognises rights of survival, development, protection and participation and an important right against discrimination. Article 2 of the Convention requires States Parties to recognise the whole range of rights in respect of all children within their jurisdiction, irrespective of the child's or his/her guardian's race, language or religion. If the articles on freedom of thought and religion or the right to pursue culture are interpreted rigidly so that they receive total priority, they will provide governments as well as adults in multi-cultural societies with a tool for undermining all the basic rights of children guaranteed in the Convention. The only way to prevent that is to develop a model for the administration of justice that relies on National Constitutions and uniform codes to forge a common legal value system that links to the international norms. Such a development will enable governments to insist that on grounds of public policy all citizens must be governed by some basic laws. On the other hand developing the choice concept in selected areas will enable minority communities to choose to opt out of their laws and utilise the uniform codes to govern their private relationships. A combination of compulsion and choice, that was familiar to legal systems with a history of pluralism within colonial society, and post independence Constitutions derived from international standards, offer some insights which are still of value today.

The basic issue of human rights and justice for children when these ideals have not been realised in the adult world, is relevant for both developing and developed countries. The concept of justice for children, developed in the Convention has been presented to the international community as a set of international human rights standards. For that very reason they link to adult rights. The concept of resource allocation, the attitude to violence in the family and the community, the rights and responsibilities of parents, and equity for the girl child, indicate that achieving justice for adults is a goal that can be realised by creating equity of children. Equity for the girl child seems to lie at the heart of achieving gender equity in a society, and yet this is a dimension that has been largely ignored in the pursuit of gender equity and non-discrimination in the last decade. A society that does not discriminate between boys and girls, provides resources for child care and development so as to support adults in their care giving roles, and protects children from violence in the home and the community must surely improve the quality of life of its adult population. Achieving justice for children is not an effort to prioritise an insignificant and trivial need, but rather a seminal effort in achieving equity and justice within a community and a nation.

Perhaps the only single area of conflict between pursuit of the goals of justice for children and justice for adults is the area of participation rights. Will recognition of participation rights for children undermine family privacy and parental authority so much that it will undermine the very foundation of nurturing and child care? Can a concept of justice that ignores parental rights and attaches importance to the child's rights of participation provide a model that has validity for countries which consider parental authority to simply a dimension of parental responsibility? The concept of the child's right to participate in decisions that affect him/her is basic to the concept of justice presented in the Convention. This basic principle is already recognised in legal systems, even in developing countries, where the idea of an age of discretion before majority recognises that legal rights expand as a child grows towards the age of majority. The Convention accepts that a diminution of parental authority and responsibility must occur as the child grows closer to adulthood, through a process of maturity and capacity for independent decision making. If this balance between parental authority and participation is maintained in legal and social policies there cannot be a conflict between achieving justice for both children and adults.

The international standard setting on children's rights has also introduced a new approach to enforcing the law and regulatory controls that is of special relevance to countries in Asia and Africa. Many countries in both these continents had traditional systems of dispute settlement that emphasised the importance of conciliation. Yet the colonial legal tradition emphasised that legal rights should be asserted exclusively in adversarial court proceedings. The concept of linkage between administrative and judicial authorities has been introduced in regard to legal proceedings involving placement of children in care. However this concept has not been really understood either by lawyers, judges or administrators, resulting in serious inadequacies in regard to administration of juvenile justice. The Convention on the Rights of the Child underlines the importance of developing a new solidarity effort between all agencies acting in matters that affect children, so the child's best interests receive primary consideration. If this provision is used to create a new environment for law making and law enforcement, legal processes may be effectively used to deliver justice to children. Judicial activism in the subcontinent of India through social action litigation shows how a legal environment can strengthen the capacity of administrators, and activists to work with the courts to realise fundamental rights guaranteed by the Constitution. Social action litigation has given activists and non-governmental organisations the status or locus standi to bring cases before the superior courts when the Constitutional rights of disadvantaged groups and children have been violated, so that positive interventions are initiated to realise legal rights. The courts have often taken on a supervisory and administrative role in ensuring that their orders are carried out. They have been able to link with the administration and even helped to initiate legislative change by using their jurisdiction in fundamental rights litigation to make orders requiring enacted laws to be brought into operation.

One of the major obstacles to using the legal system in delivering justice to children is the enactment of laws without an awareness of the diverse socio-economic supports that must be provided to make enforcement effective. The Convention adopts a holistic approach to law making and law enforcement by connecting a rights strategy with the provision of an effective socio-economic support system. Socio-economic aspects of children's rights are therefore perceived as intimately linked to realising all rights. This concept of children's justice does not maintain the familiar distinction in international law between civil rights and socio-economic rights, and recognises that both aspects must be given priority if the rights of children are to be realised. This dimension is particularly important in South Asia. Experience shows that enactment of minimum age laws to protect children against exploitation in employment or marriage are ineffective without providing an adequate infrastructure for aspects such as registration of marriage and compulsory education. Allocation of resources for these efforts must now be perceived as inevitable aspect of law making. This is why the Convention has several provisions on international and interagency cooperation in providing development assistance, and the provisions underpin articles that refer to a child's right to survival, development and protection. National plans of action must be catalyst for these efforts.

The obligation to see the realisation of children's rights as a global concern is emphasised in these articles, and they encourage a recognition of the basic reality that children's rights cannot be realised in one country without a response from others. This is seen particularly in the area of international trafficking in child labour and prostitution, intercountry adoption, and child abduction in custody cases. No amount of law making within countries where these problems occur will impact on these problems without bilateral, regional or international agreements, or willingness to conform to the international standards set by multilateral treaties. The Convention's model of justice is one that emphasises that realisation of a rights strategy for one country's children requires the commitment of others. The concept of developed countries providing assistance to developing countries is founded on the basic value that children's rights cannot be realised in countries where these are perceived as relevant only within national boundaries.

The Convention is a powerful incentive to studying comparative law developments and sharing experiences in drafting model codes that can be used in regard to a range of problems. The impact of this sharing can be seen in developments that have taken place over decades where there has been a cross fertilisation between legal systems. Indian codes of law have been transplanted to the African continent, and many countries with a common law tradition have borrowed legal concepts and principles from each other even after the end of colonial rule within countries. This kind of sharing has also taken place through the citation in one jurisdiction of judgements from another jurisdiction as persuasive judicial authorities. It has occurred through the processes of legal education and professional training. The Convention encourages the creation of a common consciousness with respect to children's rights among judges and members of the legal profession.

A common consciousness about the concepts or models of justice for children has also been emphasised in the Convention as an important priority for legislators and administrators. The lack of cooperation between administrative officials working in different branches of government has been a serious barrier to implementing law. The Convention envisages that collaboration must be developed and be treated as crucial if justice for children is to be realised.

Traditionally the courts of law and law enforcement officials have been considered the agencies entrusted with monitoring violation of rights and ensuring enforcement of regulatory controls. The Convention envisages that monitoring will be done within national boundaries by official groups such as Parliamentary Select Committees, Children's Rights Commissions or a single independent official with high visibility, such as an ombudsman. In addition, and most importantly, the community as well as non-governmental organisations within countries are seen as agencies who should be actively involved in the task of ensuring adherence to regulatory controls and official policies. The Convention emphasises that its contents as well as the regular national reports should be circulated within each country so that a national debate can be generated about a ratifying country's performance in delivering justice for children. While the traditional concept of the State's leadership role in policy-making and law enforcement has not been ignored, there is a new concept of community involvement in assisting the State to realise the legal rights of children.

Recognising the concept of community involvement in delivering justice is not a process that gives primacy to self help and extra legal action but rather a recognition that law enforcement is ineffective without community support. This can also give legitimacy to criticism and to activists and organisations monitoring violations of children's rights within national boundaries. Involvement of community workers and social welfare organisations has been traditionally recognised in many legal systems, even in developing countries, particularly in the area of administration of juvenile justice. This appears to have been strengthened through the Convention which articulates the value that legal rights cannot be realised without active community participation. Though family and parental responsibilities for children have been recognised and must be strengthened, the State, the community and children themselves have a right to ensure that children are treated with equity and fairness within the family. Similarly the community and children have a status to see that the State fulfils its commitments. This perception of the common involvement of the beneficiaries of rights in realising those rights affords a new insight into justice as a populist rather than an esoteric and unfamiliar value in a society.

CHAPTER 5

GENERAL ISSUES RELATING TO REFUGEE CHILDREN

Nyorovai Whande

INTRODUCTION

There are about 17 million refugees in the world today and three quarters of that 17 million are women and their children. Furthermore, more than half of the refugee population totally depend on international assistance for basic needs of food, shelter, water and health care. That large numbers of refugees continue to be dependent on international assistance is most disturbing. In many countries they remain in care-and-maintenance camps long after the emergency is over, denied opportunities to work or access to training or income-producing activities. They must rely on food rations, clothing and shelter as provided by international donors.

History shows that the concern for refugee women has been voiced for many years. In 1980, the UN General Assembly noted with great concern that women and children constitute the majority of refugees and displaced persons in most countries and urged the international community to provide urgent and adequate assistance to all refugee and displaced women and to developing countries providing asylum or rehabilitation, especially the least developed and most seriously affected countries.

Refugee women are affected in three ways by this international assistance system:

a) as the principal beneficiaries of assistance, they and their children suffer from its inadequacies.

b) lack of employment opportunities means they cannot provide for their families without international assistance.

c) they are seldom consulted about programmes or permitted to participate in implementation of projects designed to assist them.

What has all this to do with refugee children you may ask? I believe that we cannot deliver any kind of assistance to refugee children without including their care-givers who in most cases are their mothers. So you will have to forgive me as I attempt to go through what I think are basic needs of refugee children.

I will not deal with their needs separately from those of their mothers. Refugee children are like all children the world over in certain respects. They share a range of common needs such as physical, psychological, social, educational, spiritual and emotional which have to be met if the child is to develop normally and healthily. Refugee children are in double jeopardy, because they are children and because they are refugees. We are aware that if some of their needs are not met the consequences can be life-threatening. Unlike the children you may be working with refugee children have had to contend with a level of disruption to their individual, family and community life which few of us will ever experience. What can be more bewildering to a child than to be caught up in a war or to know that their lives and the lives of their parents are in danger. Unfortunately children do not all escape from these situations unscarred but worse still, they can continue to live with these scars unattended resulting in what we can later identify as trauma.

The following are some of the general needs of refugee children, but it should be noted that this is a summary, not an entire list.

PROTECTION

In its efforts to improve the protection of refugee children, the United Nations High Commissioner for Refugees is promoting The Convention on the Rights of the Child and is trying to come up with a strategy to monitor systematically the implementation of relevant articles.

The United Nations High Commissioner for Refugees is trying to strengthen its efforts by the following:

a)   safeguarding the priority of refugee status determination
b)   appointing guardians, legal advisers and social workers to work directly with refugee children in the camps,
c)   emphasis is being put on providing special counselling for unaccompanied minors, and giving more special training of interviewers. In addition, the Office continues to assist in arranging to place children under foster care.

The protection of refugee children should be of the highest priority to the international community. Protection is a concept that encompasses many aspects of a refugee child's life from physical safety to legal rights and a key condition of effective protection is access to the assistance needed to survive within a refugee child's context.

HEALTH AND NUTRITION

Assistance to refugee children has to go beyond the two Bs, which are BEANS AND BLANKETS. The principal cause of mortality in refugee and displaced children is malnutrition. Lack of food itself kills, and is a major contributor to death from a number of diseases. Malnourished children are more susceptible to disease and are more difficult to cure when they are ill. Malnourished women who are pregnant or lactating are unable to provide sufficient nutrients to enable their children to survive. In addition to food problems, poor sanitation and contaminated water supplies contribute to high death rates among refugee children. When basic items such as shelter, clothing and cooking utensils are not available for refugees' use the children are at risk of diseases.

Nutritional standards and the availability and quality of health care have a direct and measurable impact on the physical and intellectual development of all children. International reaction has focused on the inadequate or ill-balanced food rations which are given to refugees families and results in a steady deteriorating nutritional status for refugee children in many camps in the world. As we have all seen from the horrifying pictures of refugee children from the world over, the list is endless.

Equal access to food and non-food items is a key issue for refugee children. Decisions about food distribution are generally made by international organisations and host countries in consultation with the male leaders of the camps. Yet, these male leaders may have little understanding of the needs and circumstances of those who cook the food or feed the children, namely, the women. As a result, the food distribution procedures and contents may be inappropriate.

Physical survival is not enough for these refugee children if they are to grow up and become responsible members of society. In refugee situations, the social, cultural and psychological development of refugee children demands careful attention. The impact of war has produced more severe mental health problems for refugee children than any other known cause. UNHCR and its operational partners have a responsibility to try to identify early symptoms of trauma and to assist the refugee community in helping its children to overcome individual problems, and strengthen emotional security and stability to the extent possible.

WATER AND SANITATION

The high death rate among refugee children is related to water borne diseases. Refugee children need water of good quality and quantity. The impact of lack of water and sanitation in refugee camps means death for a lot of children. Water is related to the following activities which affect refugee children directly or indirectly.

Firstly, water distribution points far apart mean that children spend long hours in water queues and school activities cannot take place. Likewise there is little time for play or recreation. Secondly, more water means children can wash more. The link between lack of water and high incidents of skin disease is very apparent. The quantity of water in some camps means recreation for kids when the hose pipe can be sprayed for children to play in the water, thus eliminating boredom which is one of the biggest problems for refugee children - "An idle mind is the devil's workshop," Thirdly, water can enable parents to engage in some agricultural activities. This may be in small kitchen gardens but their impact on the nutritional status of the children is great.

EDUCATION

The right to education is universal. The Universal Declaration of Human Rights states explicitly "Everyone has the right to education. Education should be free, at least in the elementary and fundamental state". It is necessary to reaffirm the right of all refugee and displaced children to primary education. In particular, changes in the educational programmes should be made to ensure that girls have equal access to those programmes.

The UN Convention Relating to the Status of Refugees provides that: "contracting states shall accord to refugees the same treatment as is accorded to nationals with respect to elementary education". The problem for refugee children is when the contracting state in not even able to give its nationals any of the said education which means the refugee children cannot be expected to receive anything beyond what national children are getting.

The Executive Committee of the United Nations High Commissioner for Refugees has reaffirmed the fundamental right of refugee children to education and, has called upon all states, individually and collectively, to intensify their efforts to ensure that refugee children benefit from primary education. Yet the right to education continues to be curtailed. WHY? because the host government cannot give a refugee child education it does not have for its nationals. .

Millions of refugee children are without education, even at the elementary level. In 1987, fewer than 500,000 of an estimated 5 millions receiving assistance from the United Nations High Commissioner for Refugees were enrolled in schools. Adequate educational opportunities are crucial to the intellectual development well-being and future self-reliance of any child, while reducing trauma and despair by opening up the prospects of a better future.

The United Nations High Commissioner for Refugees' emphasis on life-preserving measures has tended to reduce the resources available for the provision of basic education to refugee children, especially in emergency situations. There is a need for an increased allocation of resources in order to address educational needs of refugee children.

In some refugee programmes the ratio of pupils-to-teacher is between 60 to 1 and 100 to 1 and sometimes higher. Most of the teachers are not qualified. Because of inadequate resources there is a high drop-out rate and a lack of women teachers which should serve as models for girls. Girls in particular have high drop-out rates because when there are no resources a girl child is the first one to be asked to drop-out. Furthermore, because custom of early marriages and traditional attitudes have a more marked impact on the education of refugee girls, female children end up with very limited options.

Access to education does not necessarily mean participation. When a mother is over burdened by house work the girl child is the first one to be asked to drop out of school in order to assist. Programmes to assist girls to stay in schools should always take account of the activities of the mother. When we have appropriate programmes for refugee women this will benefit the girsls too. Ideas to introduce appropriate technology to assist women in the long hours spent on food preparation stand to benefit the girls as well.

It is important to repeat that education is essential. We spend too much time rushing around trying to solve what we perceive as urgent. We make great efforts to save life, without ever asking what we are saving the life for. We end up indeed preserving physical life but the result may be for refugees to lead indefinite, dependent and powerless lives in the sterile environment of refugee camps. More emphasis needs to be placed on the quality of life as being of as great importance as the sustaining of life. What we do must not be driven by our own preconceived ideas of what refugees really need. We should let the refugee community reveal to us what they know to be urgent matters.

PSYCHO-SOCIAL NEEDS

Recently those who work with refugees have been discussing the impact of trauma and stress on refugee and displaced children. The discussions have taken the form of psycho-social needs of refugee children or simply the non-material needs of refugee and displaced children. Advocates for the psycho-social needs of refugee and displaced children stress the holistic approach which must be used in the healing process. They have stressed the following:

a) we must continue to address all the needs of the refugee child - material and non material;

b) we must perceive the child within the entire family and community system;

c) recognition of different cultures and how they serve to guide individuals at the intersection of a variety of associations, values and norms which govern behaviour. These in turn must be read in the context in order to have an accurate reading of trauma;

d)   trauma is not easy to measure because children are affected by situations and incidents differently and react on different levels individually. It will depend on a child's age, the family's emotional stability and the child's personality.

Moreover, the psycho-social needs of refugee children must be met in coordination with their parents' needs and understanding of the situation. In this respect the issues concerning unaccompanied children needs close attention. When parents play such an important role in the lives of children those unaccompanied children face double problems.

Unaccompanied children are those who are separated from both parents and are not being cared for by an adult who, by law or custom, has the responsibility to do so. Action to assist such children must take into account the many different reasons that may have caused them to become "unaccompanied". Children may have been accidentally separated, abducted or orphaned, they may have run away, been abandoned, or live independently with or without their parents' consent. Some children may have been sent to the country of asylum by parents who have remained in their country of origin, whilst others may be children left in the country of asylum by parents who have returned home or resettled elsewhere. Some children have been left in the country of origin by parents feeling abroad.

In yet other situations children may have been separated as a result of conscription. Different causes of separation have different implications for the care of the child and the potential for family reunion. Furthermore, the physical security and well-being of such children may be at serious risk, largely depending upon the social mechanisms at work within the refugee community to respond to their needs.

GENERAL ISSUES CONCERNING REFUGEE CHILDREN

One important area of concern is how to improve the statistical data available on refugee children. Improvement in this area means that the United Nations High Commissioner for Refugees can improve its own understanding of refugee children's needs in the field and sensitise field officers further to the importance of the protection of refugee children.

Generally there are problems linked to early marriages of refugee and displaced girls, a high rate of school drop-out among refugee girls, sexual exploitation of young girls and boys, complications from female circumcision, recruitment in the armed struggles, and problems of statelessness. In giving assistance to refugee children these must be systematically examined and more attention be paid in order to plan carefully and deliver the necessary assistance to this group of refugees.

CONCLUSION

It is fair to say that meeting refugee children's basic needs is not as difficult and complicated as we perceive it to be. The issue of refugee women can be politically, religiously and culturally sensitive. However, as we talk about issues concerning refugee children, resistance is absent and what becomes apparent is the will on all sides to give the best of assistance to refugee children. What is needed, is a good plan or policy to determine who does what and when.

APPENDIX

INTERNATIONAL INSTRUMENTS PROVIDING FOR THE RIGHTS OF CHILDREN

The 1924 Geneva Declaration of the Rights of the Child, <u>Preamble:</u> "Mankind owes to the child the best it has to give ... " <u>Principal:</u> "The child must be given the means requisite for its normal development, both materially and spiritually."

The 1948 Universal Declaration of Human Rights, Article 25(2): "Motherhood and childhood are entitled to special care and assistance..."

The 1959 UN General Assembly Declaration on the Rights of the Child, Preamble: "...the child, by reason of his physical and mental immaturity, needs special safeguards and care, including appropriate legal protection.

The 1966 International Covenant on Civil and Political Rights, Article 24(1): "Every child shall have, without any discrimination as to race, colour, sex, language, religion, national or social origin, property or birth, the right to such measures of protection as are required by his birth, the right to such measures of protection as are required by his status as a minor, on the part of his family, society and the State."

The 1966 International Convenant on Economic, Social and Cultural Rights, Article 1083: "Special measures of protection and assistance should be taken on behalf of all children and young persons..."

The United Nations Draft Convention on the Rights of the Child, Article 14(1): "The States Parties to the present Convention recognise the right of every child to a standard of living adequate for the child's physical, mental, spiritual, moral and social development."

CHAPTER 6

**MEETING AT-RISK CHILDREN WHERE THEY GET TOGETHER:
AN ALTERNATIVE CONCEPT OF COMMUNITY**

Thereza Penna Firme

WHEN MILTON DECIDED TO GO HOME

This chapter is concerned with the plight of street children. To illustrate this, I begin with the true story of a young man who had lived for a long time on the streets and eventually decided to. go home. When he was four he left home after being beaten up by his father. Then he took trains, met other kids, travelled far, until reaching Copacabana. Several times he went back home, but inbetween he stayed away, for as long as three years. He stole money and clothes while on the streets and met many kids. He was picked up several times and put into public institutions. Sometimes he was released and at other times he ran away. His father died and now he is going back to live with his real mother.

It was a critical point in Milton's life, going back home after so many years of being exposed to dangers of all sorts. He came to my door as solemn as he could be, as proud of himself as one should be, as self-confident as one would expect him to be, and told me very pompously in a farewell ritual:

"Aunty" as Brazilian children like to call any adult in a kind way, "I want to go home because I am not corrupt!"

"Great! Tell me more about this."

"Here, on the streets it is bad. Certain policemen and some guys beat me and also tell me to do bad things like stealing and other things..." (I respect his silence).

"And there?"

"There I have my mother. I want to stay with her and never come back to the street again."

"I can see how unhappy you are. Let us sit down and talk for a while. Would you?"

The conversation went on for an hour or so and Milton, a tall, 16-year old boy, expressed memories of his background, as well as a mixture of feelings of joy about going home and sorrow for leaving street friends that he could never see again, probably. He talked about many aspects of his life on the streets, which I asked him to describe:-

The group - "We spend all day talking, being together and soon we develop friendships. Nobody fights anybody. One for all and all for one. One protects the other from the police. Each one says - I will stay until a certain day; one day I will leave the street. In our group there was a guy called Paulo who used to take anyone who decided to leave the street life to the bus stop to say goodbye..."

Girls - "They seldom stayed with us on the street. They oscillate too much. I mean, that they go back and forth from street to home and from group to group. But when we have some food we take it where they are. If they get sick we try to get money and buy medicine for them. Like a family."

Food - "We pick up vegetables and fruits thrown away when the street market is over."

Bath - "There, on the seashore or at the beach. ("Do you use soap?" I naively asked). "It doesn't go well with salted water!"

Sleeping - "Cardboard on the floor. Then we move from place to place to avoid the police. This is what we have to flee from."

Policemen - "Some kick us out and away to the beach, for instance, after beating us up. Others talk to us."

Stealing - "This happens when some kids want to make use of drugs or in situations when nobody gives us food."

Violence - "Nobody ever did it in my group. If one hurts others, it is to protect himself when people react."

Rules - " Everybody follows the rules. No boss. There is respect for the one who speaks and for the one who is right. Age doesn't matter. The important thing is to respect the agreements."

The group members - "There are 12 of us, aged from 7 to 16." Milton mentioned them all, calling them by their nicknames. Nine boys and three girls. Each came from a different place very far from one another. Links were established step by step on the street corner of the busy and intense Copacabana neighbourhood.

Community - "People become like friends, get together to solve problems that the government doesn't. They decide on their own. Go after their rights, fighting."

"Your community?" I asked. "We don't have one. Here, nobody pays attention to us. Seventy per cent spit, curse, kick us. Thirty per cent come close, talk, offer food." "What counts most?" I asked. "To value us and to trust us. The majority of people think that we will steal something if we enter their house. Here the neighbours do not pay attention to us. We are like garbage blocking the way".

What is your dream? - "To possess a home. To study. To have the tenderness that I never had from a mother."

Constitution - (silence) ... "Prostitution?"

Statute - (silence) ... "Institute, orphanage?"

One week after returning home, Milton came back to tell me that he was helping his mother in the house but she insisted that he should get a job to bring money home. That was hard. Where? How? At school he had achieved only an incomplete second grade. His mother insisted and said he would get no more food until he started to work, so Milton left home and went to live with a friend. Many other street children will want to go home, hopefully. But how can they succeed and re-enter their community of origin? Is there any authentic community to absorb them as they need and deserve? And there are millions of such kids.

STREET CHILDREN IN LATIN AMERICA

Among all at-risk children, street children are probably the most visible. They are very well known in the major urban centres of Latin America (Myers and Espert, 1988). They have been the group to which welfare organisations have devoted most attention and more local projects have been established for these children than for any group of children in difficult circumstances. Nevertheless, probably no more than one percent of the region's street children receive help targeted to their needs.

Coming from poor families, these children go on to the streets in order to survive and frequently they contribute substantially to sustaining their families and themselves. Most of them return home in the evening but many sleep in the streets either because they are too far from where they live or because they experience family tensions at home. These two groups very rarely go home. A small number are totally homeless and stay in the streets for months and years. They are frequently trying to escape from violence, which paradoxically often comes from adults who should give them protection. In such situations they are especially vulnerable to malnutrition and diseases, physical and sexual abuse, exploitation of all sorts and delinquency. Although frequently suspicious of adults, they can become friends of those they come to trust. In the cities, street children are likely to meet more repression than help, because their presence in the streets is perceived as being harmful to public safety (Myers,1988).

Poverty is an important reason why children have to work or decide to leave their families. The economic stagnation of Latin American countries along with other problems such as rapid urbanisation, family disintegration and social turmoil contribute to this and so pose a permanent threat to children's rights. However, the causes of the phenomenon of street children also include severe domestic problems.

In Brazil, 35 million children and adolescents (up to 17 years old) come from very low income families whose monthly earnings are under half of the minimum wage, (less than US $50). About 7.5 million are engaged in the labour market with 40% of them aged between 10 to 14. Approximately 4 million children do not attend school. Of every 1000 students who enter the first grade, only 45 complete the 8 years of basic schooling without repeating a grade (IBGE, 1992). Finally, other sources indicate that there are about seven million 7 to 14 year-old children living on the streets of the larger Brazilian cities.

A NEW APPROACH TO CHILDREN IN BRAZIL

Attention to the needs of children is not only a question of economic development but also very much a question of political will. In Brazil, governmental assistance to disadvantaged children and youth is a relatively new initiative. In the development of public policies three main phases can be distinguished:

- The repressive-correctional phase. Born during the thirties, it essentially focused on houses of correction for adolescents who had committed offences and on vocational institutions for poor and abandoned children.

- The compensatory phase. This occurred during the 1960s (at the beginning of the military regime in Brazil) and was characterised by a conception of the child as a socially and culturally deprived person. The approach aimed to provide the child with everything that had been denied to him socially, but this turned out to be very costly and ineffective.

- The critical-structural phase. This approach coincided with a period of democratic openness in the country. Here the child is no longer seen as a deprived individual, but as the subject of his own history. It is important to ask him what he knows, what he can do. This progressively-oriented conception has not become hegemonic in the whole system; features from the previous phases continue to co-exist with the new one.

During the last phase, a whole range of new practices emerged that were geared towards overcoming the perverse cycle of institutionalisation, apprehension, selection, stigmatisation, deportation and imprisonment (Gomes da Costa, 1989). However, the implementation of a real process of change implies dismantling the old policies and putting in a new social and educational effort for the promotion and defence of Human Rights and children's citizenship.

Over the last ten years a network formed by the State, Church and voluntary agencies has arisen to attend to the needs of street children. From 1982-1983 a project on Alternative Service Programmes for street children was set up as an inter-organisational initiative involving the Brazilian government and UNICEF. From 1984-1986 the project entered a second stage through the rise of an autonomous and national movement which originated in the local community groups organised in the previous phase. The tasks were concentrated in three main areas of concern; generation of work/income, street education, and alternatives to formal schooling. In 1987 the project was divided into two major dimensions: prevention of violence and reduction of violence. Furthermore the project focused on legal reforms, reorganisation of the political and institutional system and on improving direct services for children and adolescents who are the victims of social violence. From now on efforts are being made to alter governmental institutions so that they are more responsive to the democratic process as well as to the citizen's social interests.

The old way has been denounced and a new way announced which gives children a unique status as developing persons with full protection. The key elements in this shift in perspective are:- (Figure 1)

A major feature of the 1980's was the massive mobilisation of organisational and public interests that culminated in the approval by the Constitutional Assembly (435 to 8) in 1988 of the Charter on the Rights of Children and Adolescents. Article 227 introduces into the Brazilian Constitution essential elements of the International Convention on the Rights of the Child that was approved later in 1989 (Gomes da Costa, 1991). Article 227 states - "It is the duty of the family, society and the state to assume with absolute priority the rights of children and adolescents to life, adequate food, education, leisure, occupational training, culture, dignity, respect and freedom; and in addition to save them from negligence, discrimination, exploitation, cruelty, and oppression" (Brazil's Federal Constitution, 1988).

These measures were extended by the Statute of the Child and Adolescent, approved by the National Congress and sanctioned by the President of the Republic to become law (no:8069, July 13, 1990). This Law (see Appendix 1) consolidated children's constitutional gains and revoked previous codes relating to minors. Three major results emerged from this process. Firstly there was a new legal paradigm. Secondly, the institutional restructuring included the extinction of FUNABEM (the old Welfare Program). Thirdly a National System of Distance Learning was created about children's issues. Above all, there is a permanent strong commitment to children among all the persons, groups and entities involved in the process. As Gomes da Costa (1989) says, the present and the future of the new generations is what counts most in the fight between citizenship and barbarism.

Today, more and more people have access to the discussion on children's rights. The new perception of children is not a privilege of specialists but of the entire population. The old paradigm where children and adolescents were viewed as objects of disciplinary, technical and judicial actions by the family, society and state, has given place to the new paradigm where children and adolescents are viewed as citizens with civil, social and political rights (Gomes da Costa and Penna Firme, 1990).

THE IDEALS AND THE REALITY

However, there is still a long path between the theory and the practice as experienced by youngsters like Milton, between statute on paper and statute in action, legal Brazil and real Brazil. The path has been traced but not yet followed by everyone. Omission, suppression and transgression of the rights of children and adolescents are still blocking the road to full citizenship, as in Milton's statement "we are like garbage blocking the way". The statute peeled away five hundred years of history in all directions concerning justice for children (Gomes da Costa, 1991), but the revolution must reach the real addressees. Remember, when Milton was asked what he understood by "Constitution" he replied: "Prostitution?" The three levels of power - legislative, judicial and executive - along with social movements, popular involvement and the media as a whole are pointing in the right direction but the great journey is still slow.

The Statute was passed in the midst of one of the most crucial political eras in Brazil and perhaps in the world. The 1970's were the years of Brazil's economic boom but of democratic repression; in the 1980's, the economic development began to slow down, whereas the democratic process improved; now in the 1990's the economic process is seriously disturbed while the defence of the democratic principles and institutions has reached one of its highest levels in our history Governments may collapse but the State stands up to protect democracy and justice.

A democratic nation is constructed. It starts out where popular, social and State forces come together. Communities as cells of the nation are essentially constructed. "To support children or youth in working together is, by definition, to be engaged in community development." (Hart, 1992, p.42).

Milton must go home, not alone but with community support. The experiences of togetherness in the streets had to be enforced and protected. Lessons can be learned from Milton and his companions on how to build on what is there. It is important to know which rules, which sense of power and which skills they have acquired.

CONCEPTS & PRACTICES IN RELATIONS BETWEEN STATE AND
SOCIETY IN BRAZIL, REGARDING CHILDREN & ADOLESCENTS
(Figure 1)

	NEW PARADIGM	**OLD PARADIGM**
CIVIL RIGHTS	1 children & adolescents: subjects of rights	1 children & adolescents: objects of intervention
	2 unique status as a developing person: total protection	2 object of judicial procedures
	3 open environments with to come & go	3 confinement and imprisonment
	4 right to live with family and community	4 institutionalisation with social links cut off
	5 negligence, discrimination, exploitation, and violence against children are punished by law	5 social control of violence practised by children and adolescents
SOCIAL RIGHTS	6 priority for services attending to basic needs - supplementary services - special protection services	6 compensatory / assistance services
	7 right to health care	7 deficient health care
	8 right to education and full personal development duty of parents, society and state	8 difficult access to schooling, recreational and cultural activities
	9 right to develop work abilities	9 exploitation at work
POLITICAL RIGHTS	10 decentralisation of services and fostering of community services	10 centralised services and policies

More important than returning children and adolescents to their community of origin is to bring them the spirit of community as a learning experience, to prepare the transition from the risks of the streets to the safety of any community they will help to build. Yearning for family has to be developed at the same time as the critical capacity to face family rejection. Renewed links must be considered and the revival of cultural values is essential to confront return, not as a going back but as a getting ahead, as a re-reading of the reality. At-risk children have developed their own code based on values they learned to believe in. Dismantling this is to lose the basis for constructing their community. Alternative programmes have a major role as the proper space where children and adolescents are prepared to live as community here and there, everywhere. It is the spirit of community which counts.

The purpose of such programmes is above all to stimulate children and adolescents to develop a critical understanding of themselves, their situation and society as a whole, so that they will be able to transform their own reality. A national study promoted by UNICEF in Brazil to evaluate the programmes' impact on children and adolescents (Penna Firme, Tijiboy, Stone, 1987) showed evidence of substantial changes in the psycho-social development of the children and adolescents who had the opportunity to participate in the programmes' educational and cultural activities.

Along with this alternative process which is taking place everywhere in the country, institutions must change to assure youngsters of the right to have rights, marching towards rediscovery of full citizenship for every individual during his or her entire life-span.

The expanding influence of the Statute is evident through the councils of guardianship set up all over the country. Out of 4,485 counties approximately 1,500 have installed their councils; out of 27 states 16 already have their state council. However, much remains to be done. The process is slow and slower still are the attitude changes to involve State, Family and Society. From municipality to the nation, from the family as a cell to the community, children are being given priority. 1994 will be the year of the family and it will encompass all the previous years honouring children, youth, elders, women and environment.

Around Milton - Family, State and Society must work together, as only in this way can justice be guaranteed. All the strings have to be pulled to make any sense so that going home is not to be so risky any longer for Milton and his friends. Going home is to rescue identity, citizenship, values, morality and spirituality. It is to strengthen togetherness, trust and love...hope...and faith.

Analogously, glorious will be the day when Brazil, like the young Milton, will decide to "go home" in the sense of regaining its positive forces to live with dignity.

I am grateful to the following people for their invaluable contribution in updating information presented in this chapter.

ANTONIO CARLOS GOMES DA COSTA
President , Brazilian Center for Children and Adolescents, (CBIA), Brasilia, DF

CESARE DE FLORIO LA ROCCA
President, Project AXÉ Centre, Salvador, Bahia
Consultant, UNICEF and CBIA - Brazilian Centre for Children and Adolescents

JUAN ANTONIO TIJIBOY , ED.D
Professor Federal University of Rio Grande do Sul

MARCOS ANTONIO CANDIDO DE CARVALHO
Supervisor, Street Educators, Project AXÉ Centre, Salvador, Bahia

APPENDIX 1

Excerpts from the Law no:8069
July 13, 1990

Statute of the Child and Adolescent

TITLE I

Preliminary Provisions

Art 1   This law treats of the full protection of the child and adolescent

Art 2   For the purpose of this law, the child is considered as the person who has not yet completed twelve years of age and the adolescent as that between twelve and eighteen years of age.

                In the cases specified in law this statute applies exceptionally to persons between eighteen and twenty-one years of age.

Art 3   Without prejudice to the full protection contained in this law, the child and adolescent enjoy all the fundamental rights inherent to the human person and, by law or other measures are ensured of all opportunities and facilities so as to entitle them to physical, mental, moral, spiritual and social development, in conditions of freedom and dignity.

Art 4   It is the duty of the family, community, society in general and the public authorities to ensure, with absolute priority, effective implementation of the rights to life, health, nutrition, education, sport, leisure, vocational training, culture, dignity, respect, freedom and family and community living.

The guarantee of priority encompasses:

(a)   precedence in receiving protection and aid in any circumstances;

(b)   precedence in receiving public services and those of public relevance;

(c)   preference in the formulation and execution of public social policies;

(d)   privileged allocation of public resources in areas related to the protection of infants and youth.

Art 5   No child or adolescent will be subject to any form of negligence, discrimination, exploitation, violence, cruelty and oppression, and any violation of their fundamental rights, either by act or omission, will be punished according to the terms of the law.

Art 6   The social ends towards which this law is directed, the requirements of the common good, individual and collective rights and duties, and the peculiar condition of children and adolescents as developing persons will be given due consideration in construing this law.

REFERENCES

Brazil (1988) Constituicão da República Federativa do Brasil (*Federal Constitution of Brazil*). Brasilia, Distrito Federal.

Brazil (1990) *Statute of the Child and Adolescent* (Estatuto da Crianca e do Adolescente). Law no:8069 (July 13 1990) Brasilia, Distrito Federal.

Gomes da Costa, A.C. (1989) "Infância, Juventude e Politica Social no Brasil" in Gomes da Costa et al. *Brasil Crianca Urgente*. Sao Paulo: Columbus Cultural.

Gomes da Costa, A. C. (1991) "Brazil: Children Spearhead a Movement for Change" in Black, M.N. and Light, P.(eds) *The Convention: Child Rights and UNICEF Experience at the Country Level*. Florence: UNICEF.

Gomes da Costa, A.C. and Penna Firme, T. (17-19 Dec.,1990) *Concepts and Practices in relations between state and society in Brazil, regarding children and adolescents*. Paper presented at the Consultative Meeting on the Urban Child Programme. Institute degli Innocenti. Florence, Italy.

Hart, Roger A. (1992) *Children's Participation - From Tokenism to Citizenship -* Innocenti Essays no:4, Florence: UNICEF - International Child Development Centre.

IBGE (Instituto Brasileiro de Geografia e Estatistica) (1992) *Criancas e Adolescentes - Indicadores Sociais*. Volume 4.

Myers, W. (1988) *Lighting Dark Corners: What Works - Practical Insights from the Alternative Services for Street Children Project 1982 - 1986*. Evaluation Report (unpublished). Brasilia: UNICEF.

Myers, W. and Espert, F. (1988) *Situation Analysis: Children in Especially Difficult Circumstances* Outreach Series, no:1 UNICEF/Latin American and Caribbean Region. Bogota.

Penna Firme, Thereza; Tijiboy, Juan A. and Stone, Vathsala I. (1987) *An Evaluation of the Impact of Alternative Service Programs on Street Children* (Translated from Portuguese by Henry Stone). Research Report (unpublished). Brasilia: UNICEF.

CHAPTER 7

THE LEGACY OF THE PAST ON SYSTEMS OF CARE FOR SEPARATED CHILDREN

John Triseliotis

INTRODUCTION

The aim of this paper is to identify and try to explain historically the evolution of new systems of care for children separated from their parents and how the past influences the present. In doing so, the paper will be drawing on examples from different European countries, particularly Romania. Suggestions will also be made on how improvements can come about. This largely Eurocentric approach is simply related to the writer's ignorance of sources of material relating to the evolution of child care systems in other continents. Though certain common threads can be identified in the systems of a number of European countries because of past legacies, no claim can be made of a shared history of child care. This stands to reason as ideas and systems of child care are shaped and influenced by local socio-economic conditions, ideologies, religious beliefs and value systems.

Though influences do not go singly, nevertheless it was mainly religious considerations that turned monasteries into part children's institutions some 17 centuries ago and also led to the establishment of children's homes at about the same time in the Byzantium. It was religious revivalism too that was largely responsible for the setting up of many philanthropic organisations and of a large number of children's institutions in Britain about 130 years ago, all aiming 'to save' children from 'the bad influences of parents'. In contrast, it was the appalling death rate in Foundling Hospitals and financial considerations that led to the development in many European countries of a formal fostering system, only to be abandoned for ideological reasons in some Eastern European countries in the 20th Century. It was for ideological reasons too that the introduction of foster care was delayed in England compared to Scotland, because of fears that it might undermine the Poor Law test of 'less eligibility'. (The concept of 'less eligibility' was meant to make public provision less attractive as it might weaken families' responsibilities towards their children.) It was equally Ceaucescu's ideology that resulted in something like 200,000 children being placed in Romanian Homes while an anti-abortion law was in effect and social benefits extinguished. (These points are expanded later on in this chapter.)

BACKGROUND

Instances of neglect or abuse of children, or the need to provide for them outside their own families, is not new. Throughout human history there have always been examples of infanticide, parents abandoning, selling, or placing their children in institutions or with other families because they were unable to bring them up themselves. Poverty as the key underlying factor was as real then as it is today. No doubt behavioural factors have played some part, but the predominant one is appalling poverty and destitution. As an example, the number of children abandoned in monasteries and churches during the Middle-Ages usually declined sharply during periods of prosperity. More recently the number of children surrendered for adoption in Western countries has decreased substantially with growing prosperity and higher levels of social provision for single parent families.

In the same way that some parents will kill, expose or abandon their children, caring or looking after other people's children has also been a characteristic of the human race for millennia. Different systems of caring for separated children have evolved over time, but one common thread has been the move from informal to more formal arrangements, either based on institutions, the community or both. The common characteristics in relation to residential care within Europe date back mainly to the Byzantine influence. In the case of fostering, whilst a number of countries moved from informal to more formal systems, some time ago, others are only just beginning to do so.

It is the writer's view that all systems of substitute child care become obsolete once they fail to provide compensatory experiences for the children they care for, to make up for at least some of their losses and deprivations. It is these compensatory experiences which partly enable some children to survive later adversities whilst others succumb. The compensatory experience itself is usually relative to the period and conditions of a particular country or place where it is taking place. In other words, we cannot judge the advantages of a residential resource to children in Romania or Somalia today by examining it simply through British expectations and conditions. No doubt compensatory factors interact with constitutional and environmental ones to produce survivors and losers from similar-type life experiences in ways that we do not yet fully comprehend. We know, for example, that good quality substitute family care in the form of adoption or permanent foster care can help children reverse earlier distressing and psychologically traumatic experiences (Tizard, 1977; Triseliotis, 1983; Triseliotis & Russell, 1984).

The writer's interest in exploring the influence of past legacies on present child care systems arose from visits to a number of countries and more recently to Romania. In the aftermath of the fall of the communist regimes in Eastern Europe, and particularly the fall of Ceaucescu in Romania, television treated us to distressing pictures of children of all ages in large and impersonal institutions, lacking individual attention, play or stimulation. There was no doubt about the suffering, in conditions which would have been considered unacceptable for animals in Britain. Yet the continued publicity proved to be a double-edged sword. Whilst it secured charitable contributions from different countries that helped considerably to alleviate some of the distress, it also conveyed the impression that the people of Romania were uncaring, thus attracting the attention of the powerful inter-country adoption lobby.

It is interesting to ask why the same world-wide spotlight did not focus on other countries with almost equally distressing children's institutions. For example, worse conditions have existed in some of the residential nurseries for black children in South Africa. Again not because the staff were uncaring, but through being starved of funds by the South African Government. Black residential nurseries received only about one-seventh of the government subsidy that went to residential nurseries for white children. Cynics might say that the Romanian children were white whilst the South African ones were black. Almost equally distressing conditions existed in Italian residential homes and nurseries until about 10-15 years ago before measures were introduced to begin to do something about it. Until the very recent past, Israel, like the former Soviet Union, favoured residential institutions and Boarding Schools partly on ideological and partly on pragmatic grounds. In 1987 there was considerable publicity there, but not world wide, about 'the poor and abusive conditions' for 8,000 children. Because of under-staffing many Homes were overcrowded with up to 30 children in a group having only two staff members or even one (Veerman, 1989). The Curtis report of 1946 revealed a bleak picture of residential institutions in Britain whilst in the past few years we have had the Pindown scandal in Staffordshire and the exposure of children to sexual and physical abuse in a Leicestershire Children's Home.

Whilst recognising that problems in residential care are widespread care is needed to avoid appearing to be an apologist for bad practices anywhere. No-one can defend a regime, such as the Ceaucescu one, which indoctrinated its people with the ideology that any child born with any physical or mental disability, however small, was useless to Romanian society. Even the slightest squint in a child could result in it being sent to an institution for 'incurables'. Some of the institutions were hidden in distant villages known to very few and the 'carers' encouraged to look upon the children as 'animals'. Children were found to be sharing beds and mattresses soaked with urine. In one such institution children were fed from 'one dilapidated bucket with one spoon' (Cook, 1992). The obvious difference between Romania and the other examples was the intentionality of the regime to expose children to such suffering.

A large part of the child care problems and distressing conditions in residential nurseries and homes in some Eastern European countries mainly resulted from the pursuit of ideology, but ideology was not the whole story. Part of it has also to be seen in its historical context, which was not different from that of other

European countries. Many countries in both East and West relied, until very recently, on residential care as the almost exclusive method for looking after separated children, including infants and toddlers, against all empirical evidence about its harmful effects. The factor that influenced child care policy in these countries is well known, i.e. the communal raising of children undermines individualism and promotes inter-dependence and allegiance to the group and the state. Such a conceptualisation of children's needs and remedies ascribes little or no importance to the empirically-tested concepts of separation and loss, attachment and bonding which have been influencing Western child care theory and practice over the last 40 or so years. Based also on the writer's discussions and observations in Romania, concepts such as those of the child's need for continuity of care, security, sense of belonging and identity received little recognition. Neither was it recognised that social and emotional factors could influence behaviour. This was exemplified by the way that most children's behaviour was attributed to medical or hereditary conditions. As collective rearing was seen to be the perfect state response to the needs of separated children, to acknowledge that many of their needs and much of their behaviours could be related to emotional, psychological or social factors, would have been unacceptable.

In line with this thinking, the criteria for the admission of children to residential centres were almost exclusively medical, disguising the fact that the great majority of them were admitted simply because their parents could not support them. Such an admission would again have been ideologically unacceptable. In Romania, the problem was exacerbated by the family policies pursued by the Ceaucescu regime which, whilst prohibiting all forms of contraception or abortion, also withdrew in the eighties many of the available safety nets that might enable single parents or those with large families to keep their children. Considering the hardships faced by many parents and particularly single mothers, it could be argued that it was a responsible parent who, when unable to maintain his or her child put it into an institution. Judging also by the number of children who were subsequently reclaimed, it seems that many poor parents came to view institutions as providing a service; that is as a place where they could leave their children when in difficulty and pick them up later. The fact that only about half of them were usually able to do so is not necessarily an indication of uncaring attitudes, but largely of continuing economic adversities and of changing social and personal circumstances.

As already said, ideology alone cannot wholly explain the reason for the exclusive use of institutions for substitute care in countries, mainly in Eastern and Southern Europe, which contrasts with the much greater use of foster care in Britain and other Northern European countries. Very young children are still to be found in the residential nurseries of the first countries. A mixture of historical, religious and cultural factors all seem to have contributed to this. Neither was Eastern Europe monolithic in its response, as both Poland and Yugoslavia had developed viable fostering schemes from the start of the century. Initially these were long-term placements for infants but, more recently they evolved to include, temporary care, the payment of foster carers, specialist foster carers and the provision of some form of supervision. In fact, at one stage, fostering systems in these two countries were more advanced than those of Italy.

THE HISTORICAL LEGACY

Whilst ideology may have played an important part in shaping the substitute care of children in many Eastern European countries, the historical legacy cannot be ignored. Recorded evidence about the fate and care of 'unwanted' children goes back more than 3,000 years (Boswell, 1991). The early methods for dealing with 'unwanted' infants were largely infanticide, exposure to perish or rescue by a kind stranger and, for older children, to be sold as slaves. In present day language this was a form of family planning or family limitation. Like today, the main reasons that led parents to such actions were mainly economic. The stories of Oedipus, Moses, Romulus and Remus, Daphnis and Chloe, are all illustrations of the system of exposure of unwanted children which was very widely pursued, but equally they are examples of what Boswell (1991) calls the kindness of strangers who sometimes rescued such children. Almost every country's history has heroes or tragic characters who were abandoned, to be reared by strangers.

It has been claimed, but no references could be traced, that the Romans on arrival in Britain expressed admiration that the Celtic nations did not expose their children to die as was the practice in Rome. Though evidence of exposure and infanticide in subsequent centuries is not missing, one explanation that can be offered for this possibility is that infant mortality was possibly much higher among the Celtic than Mediterranean nations. Because of this and greater insecurity from attacks and raids, parents would want to preserve any children that survived beyond birth. Boswell (1991) provides evidence showing that before the 12th century at least, there was no widespread opposition to abandonment in Europe and that it was common among the Irish and the English at the time 'and not considered sinful until the 13th century' (p. 290)

A) THE RISE OF INSTITUTIONS

It was largely because Christianity from its early years took a stance against exposure and the sale of children that some practical alternatives had to be found for the care of unwanted children. Adoption, informal fostering and later children's institutions all emerged out of the practice of exposure, abandonment and the sale of children. They continued to co-exist for centuries down to the present time.

As is often the case, an institution that is conceived for one purpose may come eventually to serve a different one. This happened to monasteries from about the 4th century A.D. Mainly as a result of patronage from the Byzantine Emperors, monasteries and monastic orders were beginning to mushroom in Byzantium, Asia Minor, Greece and other places in the area. Gradually, monasteries were also becoming the obvious places where orphans, unwanted and sometimes wanted children would be left by parents. This was explained as an offering to God, in the knowledge also that the children would receive shelter, food and education. The subsequent extensive use of monasteries in many European countries for the same purpose, came to be known as the system of 'oblation' and the offered children were called 'oblates' (Boswell, 1991). The inabilities of monasteries to respond to the need of all unwanted children was followed in the 5th and 6th centuries with the establishment of separate children's institutions in the Byzantium. It is claimed that one such institution was so big that you needed a whole day to go round it (Constantelos, 1968).

The available accounts of early institutions provide a very good example of both the operation of compensatory experiences and also of their relativity. A major compensatory factor which operated then was the provision of education. At a time when education was at a real premium, the institutional children were equipped with a form of education that was largely unavailable outside and was also in great demand. The possession of education conveyed self-esteem and opened the doors to some of the highly respected professions of the time and to the seats of government. From all accounts, and unlike today, the residents of the institutions did not carry stigma, but on the contrary some privilege was attached to those who experienced life in them. Former residents occupied very important positions in the administration of the Empire and also became bishops and archbishops. But there was another big compensatory factor. In about 550 A.D. by a degree of Justinian, abandoned children were to be free, in an Empire where much of the population was of servile status (Boswell, 1991).

The Byzantine experience has parallels with the modern British private school system. The apparent harshness and depriving experiences recorded by many of those who experienced the British private school system appeared to be compensated by the privilege and prestige they confirmed on their former pupils and continue to do. The parents who send very young children to such schools are not ignorant of all the modern theories of child development, but they must think that the compensatory factors of privilege outweigh the disadvantages.

Monasteries in Western Europe were the predominant system of child care for many centuries, until they were gradually replaced by children's institutions, convents and foster care. The monastic orders that were formed in Celtic Ireland, Scotland and Wales around the 5th Century were like communes offering companionship, protection and support to whole families. Like monasteries on the continent, they too established a long tradition of offering education to many of the young people. It was not only unwanted or orphan children that found themselves in monasteries, but wealthy families too would make use of them. The nobility would send at least one child to a monastery to obtain education and the privileges it then conferred. It has been suggested that monasteries and institutions took the problem of unwanted children out of public view and made it invisible (Boswell, 1991). Ceaucescu may have had similar considerations in mind when he expanded residential institutions in Romania. For example, some of the institutions for children with handicaps were located in distant and inaccessible places.

By the 14th century, monasteries were themselves gradually being replaced by convents and institutions for older children. Like monasteries, convents continued to provide cheap care for children but the system itself was perhaps responsible for holding back the diversification of residential care and the development of foster care. Philanthropists too during the next few centuries preferred to see their funds go into bricks and mortar in the form of large institutions. Remnants of these forms of care still remain in some European countries, whilst in others they have been abandoned or broken up into smaller units. It would be too much to claim that the move from monasteries to convents signalled also a change of focus from instrumental to more expressive values.

Because the care of infants was well beyond the capacity of monasteries by the 14th Century the more progressive cities of Italy, Germany, and France were establishing so-called 'institutes' for 'abandoned' children. Other European cities were to follow soon. As Boswell (1991) adds:

"It was in the turbulent, decadent and creative Italian city-states that the most significant early modern development in the handling of abandoned children first took hold, and from which it spread like Renaissance art and literature to the rest of Europe" (p. 426-427).

Foundling hospitals sprang up in almost every big European city including the Foundling Hospital in London in 1739 and the Glasgow Town Hospital about the same time. The minutes of the General Committee of the Foundling Hospital in London record that 'the grievance intended to be remedied by the Hospital was to prevent the frequent murder committed on poor miserable infants by their parents to hide their shame'. Whilst the scale of these institutions was subsequently curtailed, in some countries they still survive in the form of residential nurseries. The later demise of the big foundling hospitals was largely due to the unacceptable high death rate prevailing there. In one foundling hospital in Paris that catered for 9,000 infants, one-third of them died within days and before they could be moved out to foster parents (Davenport-Hill & Fowke, 1889).

Following the abolition of monasteries by Henry VIII, Britain, unlike other Continental countries, took a somewhat different route to the care of separated children. The abolition of the monasteries not only exposed the absence of a safety net for the very poor and led to the creation of the Poor Law in 1536, but also left a vacuum for the education of the children of the nobility. Whilst the Poor Law and its institutions came to confer stigma, which is still with us today, the private school system developed to meet the needs of the powerful and privileged. Since then, and until the end of the Second World War, the fate of orphans, destitute and neglected children in Britain has been closely linked to the Poor Law. The law itself viewed any services provided to the poor as a form of control rather than a service. In 1834, the Poor Law provided for the separation of children from adults, but as late as 1946 the Curtis Committee still found children alongside adults in Poor Law institutions.

Religious revivalism in Britain, North America and Australia during the second part of the last century was to lead to the formation of many philanthropic organisations, who saw it as their mission to save children from so called 'bad' or 'immoral' parents. Children's institutions proliferated all over the country and the public sector created its own industrial and reformatory schools. What was characteristic of this period was the severance of contact between parents and children. Concepts of restoration did not largely emerge until after World War II. With few exceptions, institutional and foster care were meant to last for the whole of childhood.

Following World War II, large institutions in Britain were gradually replaced by Family Group Homes, before the recent move towards small specialist units. The pace of change, though, has varied widely between different European countries. Some countries are still trying to create smaller omes and/or stop the use of residential nurseries for infants and very young children. This has also meant slowness in introducing alternatives to residential care, such as foster care. In Britain, institutions are now largely reserved for adolescents, whilst foster care has become the predominant method of temporary and sometimes permanent care for all children under five and frequently for those under 10.

B)   INFORMAL AND PRIVATE FOSTER CARE

The exposure and abandonment of children by their parents in the hope that someone would rescue them and bring them up, continued after Homeric times and it did not stop with the establishment of monasteries or children's institutions. It was common practice for parents to leave their children in or outside churches and institutions, a custom that continued in some countries until this century. An equally common practice was to leave the children outside the homes of families who were childless, wealthy or both. Parents would sometimes watch to see who picked up their child. In a small and less mobile world it was easier for parents to know who was rearing their child. Whilst some children may have been brought up well, relative to the conditions of the period, others were mainly used as service labour. Some parents not only knew which family was rearing their child, but they would also maintain contact. Parents who later reclaimed their children were expected to meet the expenses incurred by the foster carers. Like now, 'tug of love' cases were not unknown then.

A more formal kind of paid or private fostering emerged in Germany around the 11th or 12th centuries practised mainly by wealthy families who would place sons or daughters in other households and reclaim them later, usually in adolescence. A type of informal fostering was also practised in Nordic and Celtic countries involving the placing of children in each others' families. Dispersing the children in this way possibly guaranteed the survival of some from attacks, plundering and raids. The word 'alumni', so widely favoured by universities when referring to their former graduates, especially when they inundate them with begging letters, was used in the middle ages to refer to children in foster care!

If the system of oblation was a religious response to lighten the weight of those with large families and 'save' unwanted children, semi-formal fostering was expanded in the 19th Century as a response to the needs of the new British Commonwealth and its rural economy. It did not take long for some philanthropic organisations and the Poor Law authorities in Britain to recognise that they could transport many children from their residential establishments to the colonies of Canada and Australia. With no concept and programmes for restoring children to their families, cheap ways had to be found for emptying institutions. In Barnardo's words:

"A rescue Home must be continuously gathering in fresh inmates, else it would in a single generation be compelled to give the signals of retreat and close its doors, and write up in the face of new applicants: 'no admission'. But to secure the open door in front it must maintain its exit door in their rear." (Original emphasis). (Parker, 1991, p.24).

The rural economies of the new colonies run by expatriate settlers required cheap labour to work on the land. The children of the institutions in Britain were to fulfil this purpose by being shipped to the Colonies and farmed out, often without their parents' consent or even knowledge. They were placed with farming foster families. Usually there was no payment involved nor any proper form of supervision. Available accounts suggest that whilst some children, as is always the case, found caring families, many others were harshly exploited. This system of fostering overseas reached its peak in the early parts of this century, but more than one voluntary organisation continued the practice until the mid-1950s. Foster families who asked no allowance, or the absolute minimum, were seen as suitable and the opposite was seen to be true if an allowance was expected. Some of these legacies about pay and suitability have not altogether vanished.

Orphanages in the USA followed a similar practice to statutory and non- statutory agencies in Britain. Responding to the needs of their rural economies, children from orphanages were placed with foster families, mostly without pay, except for about 10 per cent of them where some payment was involved (Jones, 1989). With the mechanisation of farming, urbanisation and outside employment for women, informal and semi-formal fostering held few attractions any more for farm owners. Neither did it have, if it ever did, many compensatory benefits for the children. As evidenced by the amount of public outcry and commissions of enquiries that were set up to examine child emigration, children were on the whole having a rough deal and the expected returns were not materialising. For reasons outlined above and because of increased regulation, semi-formal fostering eventually had few attractions for carers either and there was no incentive to take on children without pay. Gradually the emphasis shifted towards paid foster care to encourage recruitment. Formal fostering from then on was beginning to assert itself.

C) THE EMERGENCE OF FORMAL FOSTERING AND PROFESSIONALISATION

Formal fostering denotes types of legally sanctioned arrangements by which non-related and sometimes related families undertake for payment or an allowance to care for someone else's child. The arrangement is supervised and except in cases of permanent fostering, the eventual aim is the reunification of the child with its original family.

This definition begs a number of questions, but it helps to distinguish formal from informal fostering which is still practised in certain countries between relatives and friends. The emphasis on temporariness and on reunification are intentional because until the end of World War II foster care was mostly practised as long-term, with no concept of reunification with the family of origin. It may now seem the obvious thing to do, but the religious revivalism referred to earlier and other ideas about what is good for children, particularly the urge to save them from the so-called 'bad influence' of their parents, did not encourage reunification.

As far as one can ascertain, formal paid fostering was an off-shoot of the Foundling Hospitals originating in France probably around 1450 and being improved at different stages since then (Davenport-Hill & Fowke, 1889). This form of formal placement was meant for infants moved out of the huge residential nurseries and placed with 'wet nurses'. Infants were placed, mainly in the countryside, with foster carers who were paid by the State and who were expected to keep the children at least up to the age of 12. The State, though, retained parental responsibility until the children were 21. Parents would sign their children to the State and if they reclaimed them later they had to meet the expenses, something improbable for most parents. However inadequate judged by present-day standards, nevertheless a system of selection and state supervision was in operation. It is claimed that most of the children were happily absorbed within their foster or adoptive families. In spite of its pioneering element, the French system was somehow slow to evolve to incorporate concepts of temporariness and restoration. Germany and other countries, including countries in Eastern Europe, took up the idea of 'wet nurses' in the latter part of the 19th Century.

The system of 'wet nurses' was equally adopted in Britain, but the children would be called back from them by the age of four to be placed as apprentices. For reasons difficult to explain, the idea of wet nurses and fostering did not appear to catch on in countries such as Italy and Greece and only in a small way in Spain. There almost total reliance was placed on residential nurseries until the very recent past. One possible explanation for this is the strong extended family systems prevalent in these countries. In such systems the boundary line between members of the extended family appear very loose allowing for the care of related children, but the boundary between the extended system and the outside world is rather rigid, leading to some reluctance to look after non-related children. Another possible explanation is larger families leaving little space for someone else's child. Recent consistent efforts in some of these countries have, however, shown that foster families can eventually be found, but it takes time and effort. This partial success may have also been aided by the changing family and socio-economic conditions in these countries, tending to facilitate the inclusion rather than exclusion of strangers' children.

If wet nursing was one kind of formal fostering, there was a second one which emerged somewhat later for older children. As far as it could be established, this type involved some selection, payment and supervision and emerged in Ireland around 1832. Religious considerations were apparently the main motivation as well as concern about the fate of 'pauper' children. The initiative was associated with Irish Protestants who, being a minority in a predominantly Catholic country, could not have viable children's institutions. Paid fostering was also thought to be preferable as it provided, in their view 'a family type rearing' (Davenport-Hill & Fowke 1889).

The Borough of Paisley in Scotland was the first to introduce family fostering in Scotland in 1838 though it was another 70 or so years before humanistic psychology was to begin to highlight the emotional needs of children. Yet awareness of these needs are to be found in the minutes of the Borough of Paisley who in adopting the Irish system of paid fostering said in their report:

> 'We believe that children brought up in public institutions, when at length turned out into the world, are, as a general rule, feeble in body and mind, and less able to fight their way through life than those who come from the common walks of life.' (Quoted by J Henley, 1870)

At this time foster placements usually involved no further contact between the child and the original family. The concepts of temporary foster care and of reunification were practised only to a limited extent in Britain until the introduction of the Children Act, 1948 and the establishment of Children's Departments. Many other European countries are still struggling with this notion. Other Scottish Parishes followed Paisley during the next 20 or so years. The popularity of fostering in Scotland may be attributed to three factors: First, unlike England, in Scotland there were fewer workhouses and out-door relief under the Poor Law was extensive. Second, fostering was found to be cheaper than keeping children in institutions. Thirdly, it was seen as more humane.

These arguments are not very different from today's, though some would challenge whether foster care is much cheaper than residential provision when the full costs are taken into account. In Anderson (1871) we also possibly have the first study of foster care anywhere. He followed up 320 children placed by the Parish of St Cuthbert's in Edinburgh and he declared the system a success, adding that it is 'the nearest approach to the family circle'.

As already pointed out, in England this form of fostering was initially resisted because of the fear that it would undermine the concept of 'less eligibility'. There was also the view that as residential homes were available, it seemed preferable to keep them full. Eventually, the Scottish system was seen to be successful and so copied. The experiment of boarding-out children with families in preference to institutional care was also taken up in New South Wales in 1872 by a Mrs Clark who became dissatisfied with the poor 'morale' of children growing up in one of the local institutions (Davenport-Hill & Fowke, 1889).

Benefiting from the experience of Sweden, professional or treatment forms of fostering were introduced in Britain in the early 1970s. During the next 20 years specialist fostering schemes were set up by most social work (services) departments. Though the success of the early programmes was not repeated, nevertheless some agencies started moving towards a fully professionalised fostering service. The term 'professional' or 'treatment' fostering is used to describe carers who are recruited on the payment of fees rather than allowances, are prepared and trained and expected to take children presenting emotional or behavioural difficulties and those with handicaps or disabilities. This was a decisive shift from the previous practice of fostering only children with no unusual difficulties.

LESSONS FOR EASTERN EUROPE

The recent move in Britain has been for policies and practices which aim to achieve permanence for children in their own families by making available a range of preventive and care measures. Permanency outside the birth family in the form of long-term foster care or adoption are reserved for a small percentage of children who cannot be cared for by their families (Marsh & Triseliotis, 1993). The preferred method for children requiring respite care or care measures is foster care, particularly for those under the age of 10. Residential care is mostly used for adolescents for whom it is also more difficult to secure foster carers. The number of children in residential care has fallen by about 60 per cent over the last 16 years (Department of Health, 1974-89).

Many recent visitors to countries such as the former Soviet Union and Romania have been asking why a system of formal foster care is not being introduced there quickly to help move more children out of institutions. An embryonic foster care system was started in Russia in the late 1980s and Romania is trying to set one up now with the aid of the Romanian Orphanage Trust (a British Charity). However, as other countries who recently introduced formal foster care have also found, such a move cannot succeed by itself but needs to be developed in association with a number of other measures, including:

First, enabling legislation which reflects largely empirically-tested knowledge about what is good for children. Much child development research carried out in the West over the last 40 years has largely by-passed not only Romania but many other Eastern European countries. Such concepts as attachment, bonding, separation and loss, including the child's need for continuity of care and knowledge about origins feature very little in existing legislation. The attitudes of many in the caring professions will also have to shift away from explaining children's behaviour too much in deterministic and almost exclusively medical and hereditary terms. A fine balance has also to be found between protecting children whilst also safeguarding parental rights and responsibilities. Rights in some Eastern European countries appear too much weighted towards parents, making it difficult to arrange formal fostering or adoption for children. It is claimed that it is far easier for a foreigner to adopt a Romanian child than a Romanian because of the antiquated laws. I am informed that the Romanian authorities are currently considering new laws on abandonment to make it easier for children to be fostered or adopted.

A second requirement is for a social work service structure staffed with trained personnel and offering suitable supportive programmemes to families and children. Compromises will obviously be necessary during the early stages until suitable staff can be trained. No services would have started anyway had they waited to have a full complement of trained personnel first. In this respect Eastern European countries could learn from the methods used in third world countries in the training of paramedics. At this initial stage, short, focused courses could respond to many of the immediate requirements.

Third, it is vital to introduce a safety net for the most disadvantaged families and children. Most nations now have a system of financial support to families including those who are out of work, sick or disabled. Romania has a system of family allowances, but apparently these are so low as to be almost meaningless. Unemployment benefit stops after a year and there is no other benefit to replace it. There is a range of other preventive measures that could be taken, including the provision of cheap day care facilities and targeted services in kind or in cash for the more problematic situations. Too many children in Romania continue to be admitted to residential institutions simply because their parents do not have enough to feed and clothe them. This is self-defeating for those trying to move say 80-100 children out to foster homes, when double that number are admitted largely because of social factors. It is claimed, for example, that more young children are entering residential nurseries in Romania now than at the time of Ceaucescu. Every time prices of stable foods rise, so does the number of new-born children admitted to Leagaries (residential nurseries). There were some ironic comments when towards the end of the last century the Austrian authorities began paying mothers for the upkeep of their own children, as if they were foster mothers, but they certainly understood something about the prevention of family breakdown (Davenport-Hill & Fowke, 1889).

Like other poor countries have discovered, there is also a real dilemma of how many of the very limited resources should go into prevention and how many into curing existing ills. The most that can be hoped for at this stage is to break down large institutions into smaller units, improve the quality of care and begin to introduce different forms of foster care with the aim of gradually closing down residential nurseries. Eventually many of the institutions for older children can be scaled down. As other countries have found this may take 15-20 years

Fourthly, some of the newly emerging countries, particularly in Eastern Europe, have lost their tradition of voluntary and philanthropic organisations which could help to complement statutory efforts. A whole generation has grown up with no experience of voluntary organisations. It was the late Professor Titmuss (1970) who remarked that if you improved, developed or adopted altruistic systems in the form of voluntary contributions, they made the people and society more humane.

REFERENCES

Anderson, W. (1871) *Children rescued from pauperism or the boarding-out system.* Edinburgh.

Boswell, J. (1991) *The Kindness of Strangers.* Penguin.

Constantelos, D.J. (1989) *Byzantine Philanthropy and Social Welfare.* Rutgers University Press, USA.

Cook, C.E. (1992) *Opening up Romanian Child Care: A study of residential policy and practice post-revolution.* Dissertation submitted for the degree of B.A., Department of Sociology/Social Policy, Sheffield University.

Curtis Report (1946) *Report of the Care of Children Committee.* HMSO, London.

Davenport-Hill, F. & Fowke, F. (1889) *Children of the State.* Macmillan, London.

Department of Health. (1991) *Health and Personal Social Services Statistics for England 1974-1989.* [Quoted by Cliffe, D. and Berridge, D. *Closing Children's Homes*, NCB, London.]

Henley, J J (1870) *Report of J J Henley, Poor Law Inspector, to the Poor Law Board, on the Boarding Out of Pauper Children in Scotland* 1871.

Jones, M.B. (1989) *Crisis of the American orphanage, 1931-1940.* Social Service Review, 63, 4: 613-629.

Marsh, P. & Triseliotis, J. (1993) *Social Work in Child Care: Prevention and Reunification.* Batsford, London.

Parker, R. (1991) *Away from Home.* Barnardos.

Titmuss, R M (1970) *The Gift Relationship.* Penguin.

Tizard, B. (1977) *Adoption: a Second Chance.* Open Books, London.

Triseliotis, J. (1983) 'Identity and security in adoption and long-term fostering.' *Adoption and Fostering*, 7, 22-31.

Triseliotis, J. & Russell, J. (1984) *Hard to Place: The Outcome of Adoption and Residential Care.* Gower.

Veerman, P.E. (1989) 'Foster families in the Kibbutzim.' *Adoption and Fostering*, No. 2, 48-52.

CHAPTER 8

THE SCOTTISH CHILDREN'S HEARINGS SYSTEM: INTERNAL
DEVELOPMENTS AND THE UN CONVENTION

Andrew Lockyer

INTRODUCTION

The distinctive Scottish Children's Hearings System was established by the Social
Work (Scotland) Act, 1968, following the recommendations of the Kilbrandon
Committee (1964). It deals with nearly all circumstances where compulsory
intervention by the state in relation to children might be needed. To mark two
decades of the system's operation, Professor Sanford Fox, who has a long
association with Juvenile Justice in Scotland, was invited in May 1991 to give the
first Kilbrandon Child Care Lecture at Glasgow University. In his lecture,
Sanford Fox referred to the Children's Hearings System as one of Scotland's
"historic accomplishments" to be compared with the creative "genius" of the
Scottish Enlightenment philosophers. He commended the vision of Lord
Kilbrandon and his committee and he praised those working within the system
who "have over the years nurtured the Hearings and brought the Scottish system
of juvenile justice to a position of well justified pre-eminence in the world's
juvenile justice systems" (Fox, 1991 pp.2-3). While acknowledging the
achievements of the hearings system, Professor Fox also identified areas where
he saw scope for improvement. He raised the issue of "legal representation" and
suggested the need for amendment here to meet the terms of the UN Convention
on the Rights of the Child.

This is a propitious moment to be critically examining the achievements and
possible shortcomings of the hearings system, because as well as external
attention to children's rights, the third decade has begun with reports from a
number of internal reviews and inquiries, which are expected to lead to new
legislation in the near future. I shall begin by giving a brief outline of the
principles and institutions of the hearings system, as they were envisaged by the
Kilbrandon Committee. I will then go on to discuss some internal developments
to see whether they require modification of the system. In the third and final
section I will discuss the external challenge presented by the UN Convention on
the Rights of the Child.

OUTLINE OF THE FOUNDING PRINCIPLES AND INSTITUTIONS

With some slight modifications, the major institutional innovations of the Children's Hearings System were the creation of the Kilbrandon Committee. However, the significance of the institutional arrangements must be understood as the product of some radical thinking about children, families, the community and the law. What is called "the Kilbrandon philosophy" is not only embodied in the existing legislation, it is the inherited ethos, or shared credo of those who work in the system. It provides a foundation of principle against which institutional arrangements are to be understood and practice is to be evaluated.

1. KEY PRINCIPLES

Separation of Proof and Disposition. The Kilbrandon Report said "the adjudication of the allegation issue and consideration of the measures to be applied", should be dealt with separately (Kilbrandon, 1964, paragraph 70). Court rules and procedures were designed for the adjudication of evidence and the determination of guilt or innocence, but did not provide a setting best suited for an open discussion of what, if any, measures of intervention are required. In almost 95% of cases "judicial finding of fact is not at issue", so the essential task is deciding on appropriate measures which requires "quite different skills and qualities". This could best take place in a different kind of forum, that of a "children's panel" hearing. This separation has been described by Lord President Hope (the senior Scottish judge) as the "genius" of the 1968 Act (Sloan v B, 1991).

The Welfare Principle. The fundamental proposition of the Kilbrandon philosophy is contained in a sub-heading of the report: "The Needs of the Individual Child as the Test for Action" (Kilbrandon, 1964, p.39). This is incorporated in the 1968 Act by adopting the child's "best interests" as the sole criterion in decision-making. Whether children or young people come to "public attention" as offenders, in need of care or protection, or beyond parental control, they should be treated alike on the basis of their needs. This was a radical step and is still perhaps the most controversial internationally, since most jurisdictions separate child care and juvenile justice. It has been argued elsewhere that this extends the conception of justice for children to include rather than contrast with welfare (Lockyer, 1982).

The Kilbrandon Committee believed that children who came to the attention of courts for whatever reason, shared a basic similarity from the point of view of their needs. In all cases "the upbringing process had for whatever reason fallen short" (Kilbrandon, 1964, paragraph 15). The manifest behaviour of child or parent which constitutes the justification or grounds for intervention is only one indicator of the need for "compulsory measures of care". It may or may not be the central concern and the focus for remedy. The paramount need is for "care"; which is defined by the Act as including "protection, control, guidance, and treatment" (Act, 1968 32(3)). Therefore, the compulsory intervention by a hearing is deemed a supervision requirement, not a sentence.

Participation of Child and Family. Another central doctrine is that decisions about "care" must be based on the consideration of the **whole child** in the context of **the family.**

The central presupposition of treatment rather than punishment is that the young person is not solely responsible and culpable for their behaviour. Those responsible for a child's care and upbringing have played some part and bear some degree of responsibility for what a child is and does. While the Kilbrandon Committee saw no virtue (nor precedence in Scots law) for holding parents legally culpable, their crucial influence must be acknowledged (Kilbrandon, 1964, paragraphs 18-33).

State intervention is justified only if the family cannot recognise or deal with "the problem". The family is the principal focus of treatment and remedy. Involving parents and children in the decision process and the treatment plan is the concomitant of identifying the problem as a collective one. A major theme of the Kilbrandon Report was partnership with parents and children in seeking to solve problems. **Participation** in the decision process was seen to be an essential component in that **partnership**.

2. THE ELEMENTS OF THE SYSTEM

The Children's Hearing. The Children's hearing was established as a decision-making tribunal which is less formal than a court. Hearings, it should be remembered, only consider disposition when the grounds for referral are accepted by all parties or have been proved in court. Denials are remitted to the Sheriff (a judge) in "closed court" and, if found proven, sent back to hearings for disposition.

The proceedings in the children's hearing are relatively informal. The rules of the hearing are designed to facilitate full, frank and informed discussion between all parties. The hearing is a round table discussion between parents, child or children, panel members, social worker, reporter and any other interested person who the chairperson deems might be helpful. There may be present a child specialist to speak about a report previously submitted, a representative of the school, neighbour or family friend: notwithstanding those with a right to be present, numbers must be kept to the minimum necessary.

The panel chairperson has the duty to ensure information in reports is understood; the views of children and parents are sought; the process and the reasons for decisions are explained; the right to appeal and seek a review is known about. The process is sometimes described as "inquisitorial" rather than "adversarial", but this is misleading as a decision model, even if it describes part of what occurs. The process is **discursive** - and ideally **consensual**: that is, it is a discussion which aims at finding common ground and seeking consensus, even if this is not always achievable.

Panel Members. It was a bold innovation of Kilbrandon to turn to the Scottish public to recruit a new category of judicial decision-makers. A mixed gender panel of 3 members hear on average 3 or 4 cases in a half day session. The hearing members are chosen to serve from amongst a lay panel of citizens selected in each region, but appointed for each region by the Secretary of State for Scotland. The dual criteria for selection to the panel were "they should have knowledge and experience in dealing with children, and should be drawn from a wide range of occupation, neighbourhood, age group and income group" (Guidance, 1969) A broad social class mix together with appropriate knowledge, skills and values has been achieved (See Lockyer, 1992, Chapters 3 and 4). Panel members must also undergo training before they serve.

Placing the decision about "compulsory measures of care" into the hands of a cross-section of the community could have a number of advantages. Lay panel members might (1) "identify" better with families, and so communicate with them more effectively by speaking the same "ordinary language"; (2) promote a "caring community" where neighbours share an interest in each other's children; and (3) make state employed care workers answerable to citizens representing the public. To what extent these aims are fulfilled, and whether they are desirable is open to debate. One view is that the public involvement gives the welfare system credibility, another is that professional child care and case planning is hampered. One of the latent functions (which cannot be bad) has been the social education and sympathetic enlightenment of a section of the Scottish public about children with problems.

Reporter to the Children's Panel. The unique office of the Reporter was at the centre of the Kilbrandon Committee's institutional proposals. The new office was set up to receive and investigate referrals from all agencies or individuals, and decide if children and parents should be brought to hearings, or whether voluntary help should be offered.

The reporter is required to determine whether there is sufficient evidence to support grounds for referral, and if there is a **prima facie** need for compulsory measures of care. Where the grounds for referral are denied, the reporter has the task of seeking to establish the grounds before the sheriff. Knowledge of the law and a capacity to perform in court must be combined with the relevant knowledge and skills to assess children and their families, normally from the reports of other professionals, but sometimes also by interview. In addition the reporter must act as clerk and legal advisor to the hearing and be responsible for defending the hearing's decision at appeal.

In practice reporters work in close co-operation with the police and the care agencies - health, social work and education. They are officers of the local authority and are dependent on the authority to meet their budgetary needs, but they retain independence of the authority in making referral decisions, and have employment protection which guarantees this independence. There has recently been a review of the Reporter's Service which considered but rejected transferring responsibility for it from local to central government: however the introduction of a central Inspectorate for Reporters is recommended (Finlayson, 1992).

Social Work Department. The Kilbrandon Committee conceived of intervention as "social education and training", therefore they proposed that dispositions would be effected through "a field organisation" as a branch of Education. The 1968 Act however gave this role to newly created local authority generic social work departments (with some regrettable loss of educational involvement in the system).

Social work departments are obliged to provide support for children to prevent them from formal involvement in the care or justice system (SW (S) Act, 1968, section 12). They have the duty to refer cases to the reporter where there might be a need for compulsory measures. They must provide reports to hearings and these normally carry recommendations. Social workers are expected to participate in hearings, and carry out panel members' decisions. The social work department is the organ of the local authority which must resource voluntary and compulsory measures of care. This involves providing a range of services to support children remaining at home, or away from home with substitute families or in residential homes and schools.

Supervision Requirements. Hearings may make compulsory supervision requirements for children residing at home, or in residential or foster care, "with such conditions as they may impose" (Section 44 (1)). These requirements must be reviewed within a year - sooner if a change is proposed by the local authority or requested by parents or children. At reviews the performance of families and social workers is scrutinised. Requirements may be terminated, changed or continued at review. No permanent decisions can be made by hearings, but supervision could be maintained with regular reviews until the age of majority. There is a general provision that a child should not remain subject to a supervision requirement "for any time longer than is necessary in his interests" (Section 47 (1)).

INTERNAL DEVELOPMENTS

In 1988, the Secretary of State established a **Review of Child Care Law in Scotland**, "to identify, in the light of developments since the implementation of the Social Work (Scotland) Act 1968, options for change and improvement in child care law...". Preliminary consultation indicated that no radical change in Scotland was required, and this was confirmed by the examination of the review group. After setting out principles which took account of the European

Convention on Human Rights and the UN Convention on the Rights of the Child, the Report concluded that "existing law was fundamentally sound and met the main needs of children and their families... there was no need for wholesale revision or restructuring", (CCLR, 1990, paragraph 1.15). The Report makes 95 recommendations, which aim to make the law "clearer and more coherent."

However, before the process of legislative reform could be put in motion, a series of further internal reviews and inquiries relating to child care took place. In the case of the two Judicial Inquiries both were precipitated by events in Scotland (Clyde, 1992; and Kearney, 1992). How far the conclusions of the Review which reported in 1990 remain valid is open to some question.

Clearly there will be some modifications to the hearings system in the legislation which is expected in 1993 or soon after. Although there remains no anticipation of fundamental change to the hearings system, there is scope for disagreement both about what would count as fundamental, and about what changes are needed. Here we can examine whether there have been developments internal to the system, which demand re-orientation of the legacy of Kilbrandon.

1. THE CHANGING PATTERN OF REFERRALS

There have been some minor additions to the law relating to hearings during the past two decades, but the main developments to date have been in practice. The major internal change to the hearings system has come from the shifting balance of child care concerns, and the practice and organisation of service provision.

The single most significant change over the past two decades has been the growing proportion of children coming to hearings as victims (or potential victims) of neglect or abuse. In the first decade after the system's introduction in 1971 the large majority of hearings dealt with children who had committed offences and truants. Referrals to the reporter for neglect and abuse in percentage terms were in single figures. Over the second decade these referrals steadily increased to become over one third of referrals to the reporter and over half those referred on to hearings. Now the majority of hearings and supervision requirements relate to cases where the grounds for referral are concerned with child neglect or abuse.

The shift in the balance of cases comes together with the organisational growth of the professional agencies who service the hearings system. Whether the changes in the balance of grounds for referral are primarily cause or effect of professional developments is open to question. They will be in some degree mutually causal. The key question is, has the nature of the hearings system significantly changed? In particular, does the hearing itself still occupy the place at the centre of the system as was envisaged by Kilbrandon?

2. INCREASED ROLE OF THE COURTS

There has been an increased involvement of the courts in the hearings system as a consequence of the shift in the balance of cases. Whereas most alleged offences committed by children are accepted, two-thirds of the abuse and neglect grounds are sent to the court for proof. The evidence in these contested cases is often complex and difficult. Although technically the hearing of evidence is before a judge (the sheriff) in chambers, the system has become more court-focused than it used to be. The concomitant effect is a greater involvement of lawyers in hearings' cases, about which there are mixed views.

The reporter has now to devote more time to presenting and preparing cases for proof. It has recently been estimated that 75% of reporters' time is devoted to child protection cases (Finlayson, 1992, p.11). The growth in court work has led some commentators to believe that a legal qualification for reporters is now essential (Kearney, 1992, p.472).

The role of the court is no longer adequately distinguished as that of determination of facts. In judging the evidence in cases of abuse and neglect the courts are to some degree involved in defining what are minimum standards of adequate parenting. What counts as "acceptable chastisement" or what amounts to "impairing health and development" are questions for the courts to determine. This takes them into the territory of defining welfare, although not determining disposition. Courts and hearings are jointly in the business of determining acceptable standards of "care". There now needs to be more mutual recognition of what each other is doing.

3. EMERGENCY PROTECTION

The increase in abuse and neglect referrals and the greater frequency with which the grounds in these cases are contested, means there are more occasions of separation of children from parents before any grounds have been accepted or proved. Justices or sheriffs authorise initial orders to permit the removal of a child to a place of safety, hearings consider the continuation of place of safety warrants as an interim measure of care, before evidence for grounds for referral is heard by the court. The present arrangements for emergency protection are widely regarded as unsatisfactory: they are probably the least satisfactory aspect of current law and practice.

The differentiation of function in emergency protection between courts, hearings, and officers is less than clear cut. The Clyde Report suggests that emergency protection orders should become the remit of the sheriff court rather than children's panels, who should only become involved after grounds for referral have been proved. This is a controversial proposal, for which it is hard to find the rationale in the events investigated by the Inquiry. The best reason for transferring jurisdiction to the court is if the decision should be based on a preliminary view of evidence. The argument for the hearing retaining the jurisdiction over emergency placements is that the decision is essentially one about where a child should be cared for, given the allegation and the views and attitudes of family members.

Whichever forum is the best location for considering emergency protection, there is need to improve both procedure and professional practice to ensure the removal of children from home is a considered judgement of last resort. There is also a valid case (identified by Lord Clyde) for enhancing the right of children and parents to challenge emergency protection arrangements.

One of the major weakness at present is that the powers conferred by warrants are too general and unspecific, which leaves the authorising agency (legal officer, hearing or court) with too little discretion and control, and the authorised agency (local authority social work departments) with too much. This in effect gives families little opportunity to question judicially what takes place under the terms of an order. Part of what is needed is the power to make warrants which can specify conditions - for example, relating to access, contact, or permission to dispense with parental consent to medical examination (CCLR, 1990). The case for such conditions would require justification, which could be challenged by family or hearing members and, if necessary, heard by the court.

If hearings retain jurisdiction over interim care they require the power to allow children home under specific conditions - like the absence from the house of an alleged abuser. Whether or not it would be preferable for the court to have a direct power to exclude an alleged abuser is a matter of on-going debate. A key question is whether this provision would enable more victims of alleged abuse to remain at home. This is an issue where Scotland might seek to learn from experience in other countries.

4. CHANGES IN PRACTICE

Developments and thinking outside Scotland have affected child care practice and services. For example the ideology of minimal intervention has influenced social work thinking about the use of compulsory measures. There is now greater diversion from hearings and more voluntary support offered to families. The use of foster care has increased relative to residential care over the past ten years, especially in the placement of young children. The shift in social work thinking has not been entirely in step with that of panel members. Some panel members express concern about their great difficulty in accessing placements which they judge to be the most appropriate for particular children. A survey in 1988 found that hearings' decisions were perceived to be "resource limited" in one in five cases (Lockyer, 1988). It also found that social workers were less likely to recommend compulsory intervention than hearings were to impose it, which was a reverse of the position found to be the case by earlier research (Martin, Fox and Murray, 1981).

There is greater potential for conflict now that local authority social work departments are active in developing their own child care policies, which have implications for the types of resources available, yet lay panel members have the ultimate responsibility for deciding on what form of care is appropriate in individual cases. Certainly in some areas there has been growing departmental control exercised over social workers attending hearings, which in one region has led to significant conflict (see Kearney, 1992).

The informal consensual model of hearings may rest uneasily with the trend to adopt corporate strategies and corporate care plans within social work departments. Local authority social workers have become to a significant degree "bureau professionals", who are increasingly the purveyors of collective departmental policy and case judgements. Individual social workers at hearings are thus more inclined to be viewed as inflexible and constrained participants - not open to influence by families or amenable to discuss alternative disposals proposed at hearings.

5. SHOULD THE MODEL OF HEARINGS CHANGE?

There has been no research to tell us whether hearings dealing with child protection grounds are significantly different from others. However, the Scottish Directors of Social Work believe that the character of hearings has changed, and this ought to be acknowledged when reviewing the workings of the system. In their paper "Child Protection: Policy, Practice and Procedure" (1992) they claim that a system primarily designed to deal with delinquency has to be modified to deal with child protection:

> "In cases of child protection a process of review and arbitration between differences is tending to replace open-ended discussion and initiation of solutions and services, which the system originally envisaged. ... Today hearings are more likely to involve adjudicating between representations being made to it, rather than more open-minded search for common ground." (6.3.3.)

The implication is that "child protection" hearings are different and this needs to be recognised, by for example, having advocates for children and parent, and a special category of panel member to deal with child protection cases.

This suggests two things: firstly, **the consensual model** of the hearing - it being non-adversarial and seeking the co-operation of the family - is inapplicable in protection cases; secondly, that it is both possible and desirable for the system to **separate "offence cases" from "protection cases".**

A False Dichotomy. The dichotomising of cases by grounds for referral is convenient for classification purposes but contentious as a basis for action: it is contrary to the welfare philosophy of Kilbrandon. The issue is whether in reality cases labelled "protection" (where the ground for referral is abuse or neglect) are systematically and significantly different from other cases. My experience of hearings is that there is no such clearcut difference, either in the range of family problems identified or in the character of hearings.

The Directors' view overlooks the extent to which complex family problems and adjudication between parents and department can be a feature of cases referred on offence grounds. Equally, I believe, they underestimate the extent to which the consensus approach is possible where grounds derive from abuse and neglect. This is not to deny that the consensual model is under strain in some cases: when, for example, one or both parents are alleged or proven abusers (and there may or may not be a prosecution pending). The Directors' characterisation fits some "hard case" hearings, but my judgement is that it is not the **norm** in cases where children are victims, and should not become the **paradigm.**

The greatest practical difference from the panel members' point of view is between cases where the agency professions have already arrived at their own consensus (at a case conference or internal review) and occasions when they have not. There is substance in the view that the arena for open ended discussion may have shifted from the hearing to the social work department's internal review. Certainly, hearings have increasing difficulty in obtaining access to specialised resources on their own initiative. This is not peculiar to "protection" cases. Where there are neglect or abuse grounds there is a higher probability of social work recommendations being accepted by hearings - over 90% correspondence (Lockyer, 1988).

The view of the hearings' role as "validating decisions" or "adjudicating between representations" is a partial description, which is a highly doubtful basis for prescription. The non-adversarial consensual model of the hearing is certainly under some internal threat. It may unwittingly be a consequence of the social work internal review becoming the consensus-seeking forum. Equally it may be a consequence of the adversarial court phase coming to dominate the mental set of social work thinking. These are not sufficient reasons why the Kilbrandon conception of the hearings' system should give way to the adversarial model.

6. THE PANEL PERCEPTION

Amongst panel members there is a strong belief that hearings ought not to be differentiated on the basis of the grounds for referral. In **all cases** the hearing's task is to ensure the child is receiving adequate care, including both "protection" and "control". A recent survey of panel members shows that there is a high degree of satisfaction with the system's capacity to provide child protection, but less satisfaction with how it deals with delinquency and children's educational needs (Lockyer, 1992).

It is fair to say that within child care services priority is given to child protection, which few would object to. This has to be at the cost of devoting less generic social work time to dealing with offending behaviour or helping meet children's educational needs. Panel members here express a concern. To remain a credible alternative to the courts, hearings must be seen to pay attention to the needs of young offenders -including their interest in avoiding a criminal life. The concentration on a narrowly conceived view of child protection runs the risk of driving a wedge to separate the deserving from the undeserving: a philosophy which the system, at its inception, set itself against.

THE EXTERNAL CHALLENGE OF THE UN CONVENTION AND REPRESENTATION

1. THE WELFARE PRINCIPLE

How does the hearings system measure up to the standards set by the UN Convention? Article 3.1 states : "In all actions concerning children the best interests of the child shall be **a primary consideration**". The Scottish system goes further in making the best interests of the child **the** primary consideration in any disposition. In fact the 1968 Act made the welfare of the child the only criterion in the justification of intervention and disposition. Although it may be argued that the interests of children must take account of the interests of others, and it is in a child's interest to be prevented from offending, the only formal recognition of consideration of others in the legislation is in relation to the use of secure accommodation (an amendment introduced in 1983), which allows "likely to injure himself or other person" as one of the criteria (Section 58A(3): See Kearney, 1987). Adoption of Article 3.1 would be a dilution of the general principle underpinning the hearings system.

However, Article 41 says:

> "Nothing in this convention shall affect any provisions that are more conducive to the realisation of the rights of the child and that may be contained in ... states' law."

Therefore, Scotland can retain the child's best interest as **the primary** consideration.

2. THE LORD ADVOCATE'S LIST

There are two categories of children who are treated outwith the hearings system and it is not clear that their treatment is in line with the convention.

The first is the class of offenders who are alleged to have committed crimes which the Lord Advocate has determined are of such seriousness that there is a public interest in them being dealt with in the adult court. These are offences such as murder, rape and other serious assaults; some lesser offences have been removed from this category in recent years. The numbers of such offenders are now quite small.

In these cases where the child's best interest is certainly not **the primary** consideration, it is unclear whether formally it is even **a primary** consideration. Moreover, the convention seeks "laws, procedures, authorities and institutions specifically applicable to children" (Article 40 (3)). The practice of dealing with the most serious child offenders in the adult court does appear to be in conflict with this article. (It should be said that every effort is now made to keep serious offenders under 16 out of custodial institutions for adults).

3. 16 - 18 YEAR OLDS

The second exception concerns 16 - 18 year olds who are dealt with in the adult court system. The UN Convention in Article 1 defines "children" as persons under the age of 18 - unless a state's law gives them "majority" (full citizen's rights) younger, which in the United Kingdom it does not.

Here the Scottish law permits but does not require compliance. A child may be subject to the jurisdiction of the children's panel up to the age of 18, but also may appear in the adult court after the age of 16. The courts have the power to remit cases back to hearings or seek the advice of hearings; and they must at least do the latter, if the young person is already subject to a supervision requirement.

In practice, it must be said, for many years the hearings system has tended to treat 16 (which is the minimum age of leaving school and a watershed of legal capacity) as the cut off point for terminating supervision and subjecting young people to the consequences of adult responsibility. There is now movement to retain more 16 -18 year olds in the hearings system. This has been spurred by the knowledge that a high number of young people who go to courts in Scotland end up in prison. There is some resistance from prosecutors, court interests and government, and the channelling of appropriate resources is a major issue. The UN Convention will lend support to those who are committed to retaining older adolescents in the hearings system.

4. LEGAL REPRESENTATION

Professor Fox in his 1991 Kilbrandon Lecture suggested an area where the hearings system is at odds with the UN Convention. This relates to lack of legal representation at the hearing. He refers us to Article 37 (d) which says:

> "Every child deprived of his or her liberty shall have the right to prompt access to legal and other appropriate assistance, as well as the right to challenge the legality of the deprivation of his or her liberty before a

court or other competent, independent and impartial authority, and to a prompt decision on any such action."

Fox invites us to consider the Scottish Place of Safety Order (used in emergency child protection) and suggests there is a gap here that needs to be filled. There is a right of appeal to the sheriff court against a hearing's decision to detain in a place of safety, which must be heard within three days and for which legal aid is available. (A deficiency not noticed by Fox is that there is no right of appeal against the initial ex parte order granted by a legal officer until reviewed by a hearing, which could exceptionally with current practice be up to seven days after removal. This lack of a timely appeal to the court is likely to be shortly remedied). However, the right of appeal to the court is not considered by Fox to be sufficient to satisfy the Convention. The fault he finds, as with so many formal children's rights, is that they presuppose children are competent actors, or exercisers of rights before the law. He invokes Sheriff Kearney who says "given the inarticulate nature of many of the parents and children involved the possibility of an early appeal to the Sheriff...may be a remedy which is more apparent than real" (Fox, 1991, p.10).

How big and how real is the "gap" which Professor Fox has exposed? His argument is that children need access to legal assistance at hearings that might deprive them of their liberty. If there is such a need, it is hard to see how this is confined to Places of Safety Orders, since all compulsory measures of care are a loss of liberty. It appears that all children must have legal representatives at every hearing to make good their real right of appeal. If Sheriff Kearney's argument is thought decisive, parents too should be legally represented. If the gap exists it is a big one, only to be filled by full legal representation of all parties at hearings.

To be coherent the argument has to be regarded as proposing a major change to the hearings system. But how convincing is this argument for lawyers to be present at all hearings? It should be noticed that the case is not grounded in the need to help a child or family member express their views, or argue for their idea of the best disposition. Presumably Fox accepts the validity of the idea of a decision forum which directly communicates with and involves family members (where "representatives" who may be lawyers are allowed, but they may not speak instead of children and parents). The case he makes for lawyers being present is that they are needed to decide for children (or help them decide?) whether to appeal against hearings' decisions. Why is it not sufficient that family members are told they have this right and may have the help of a lawyer if they wish to exercise it?

It appears to be necessary to have lawyers in hearings to note any procedural deficiencies that might provide the basis for an appeal. This line of argument would seem to warrant children and (some) parents being accompanied by lawyers in all dealings with officialdom (at least where vital interests were involved). However, in a hearing both the hearing chairperson and the reporter have a direct responsibility to take care of the child's rights in the proceedings. The likelihood of a successful appeal on a narrow procedural issue is extremely remote. The courts (sheriff and court of session) have been very unwilling to overturn welfare dispositions on procedural technicalities at appeal. The additional rights protection afforded by Fox's proposal, on the basis upon which he argues for them, may themselves be "more apparent than real".

The problem for the Scottish system, if there is one over legal representation, is that the UN Convention presupposes that children subject to the penal law will be dealt with by courts. Professor Fox (who observed at Geneva) has told us that the drafters were not required to consider the Scottish system, because the UK delegation were ignorant of it.

5. THE UNITED KINGDOM RESERVATION

It may be that the British government has been more convinced by Professor Fox than I have been, or else they are being cautious. The UK instrument of ratification of the UN Convention contains the following reservation:

> "...Legal representation is not permitted at the proceedings of Children's Hearings themselves. Children's Hearings have proved over the years to be a very effective way of dealing with the problems of children in a less formal, non adversarial manner. Accordingly, the United Kingdom, in respect of Article 37(d), reserves its right to continue the present operation of children's hearings."

The above shows the clear determination of the UK government to retain the Scottish system of juvenile justice intact. (Incidentally, it also illustrates one of the problems of the application of universal standards to atypical institutions.) However, this is to my mind a too defensive strategy. If current practice is to be defended, I would prefer that it be grounded on acceptance of Article 41, the "higher standards" provision (see above).

This would require people in Scotland to show that legal representation before the courts, in relation to proofs and appeals, was sufficient. Having Children's Hearings without lawyers being needed to speak for children and parents, would have to be shown to demonstrably enhance the direct **participatory rights of children** (endorsed by Articles 9.2, 12.1 and 12.2). Hearings might also be seen to enable the fulfilment of the rights and responsibilities of parents (endorsed by Article 5) by not only permitting but requiring their participation. This is not to say that the hearings system is necessarily superior to other legal systems in its delivery of children's rights. It is only to suggest that it may be, or have the potential to be, even if only part of its decision-making institutions attaches importance to legal representation.

6. CONCLUSION

The acknowledgement of the importance of rights does not resolve the question of where the balance is to be struck between specific entitlements or types of rights. In the case of children the proper balance between rights of agency and rights of recipience, or between liberty and paternalism, is notoriously unstable and difficult to judge; where it lies must vary between individuals and for the same child through time. This alone makes any universal declaration of children's rights necessarily fluid and open to interpretation, quite apart from the putative need to acknowledge different cultural norms. Therefore, as a check-list of criteria for assessing a state's institutional arrangements, the Convention might turn out to be of limited value.

However, what it should do is provide a general framework for looking at how children are regarded and treated under a state's law. What can be asked of any set of institutions dealing with children is that they require adults to be child-focused. To do so, I think, they must at least promote consideration of children's developing autonomy as part of their interests, and also encourage constant openness to re-appraisal. The Kilbrandon philosophy of the hearings system in principle meets the requirement of being child-centred, but remaining self-critical about how its institutional embodiment meets the legitimate interest of children is a matter for continuing vigilance. The provisions of the UN Convention on the Rights of the Child, if regarded collectively as a normative standard, are relevant to law and practice in Scotland as elsewhere.

REFERENCES

Association of Directors of Social Work (1992) *Child Protection: Policy, Practice and Procedure*

CCLR (1990). *Review of Child Care Law in Scotland: Report of Review Group appointed by the Secretary of State.* Edinburgh: The Scottish Office, HMSO.

Clyde, Lord (1992). *The Report of the Inquiry into the Removal of Children from Orkney in February 1991.* Edinburgh: HMSO.

Finlayson, A. (1992). *Accountability.* Edinburgh: SWSG, The Scottish Office, HMSO.

Fox, S. (1991). *Children's Hearings and the International Community. The Kilbrandon Child Care Lecture.* Edinburgh: Scottish Office, HMSO.

Guidance (1969). *Social Work Services Group Guidance* (to Children's Panel Advisory Groups) No: SW/7 1969.

Kearney, B. (1987). *Children's Hearings and the Sheriff Court.* Edinburgh: Butterworths.

Kearney, B. (1992). *The Report of the Inquiry into Child Care Policies in Fife.* Edinburgh: HMSO.

Kilbrandon, Lord (1964). *Report of the Committee on Children and Young Persons. Scotland:* Cmnd. 2306, HMSO.

Lockyer, A. (1982). Justice and Welfare. In F. Martin & K. Murray (Eds.), *The Scottish Juvenile Justice System,* 176 - 190. Edinburgh: Scottish Academic Press.

Lockyer, A. (1988). *Study of Children's Hearings' Disposals in Relation to Resources.* Children's Panel Chairman's Group, Edinburgh, Macdonald Lindsay.

Lockyer, A. (1992). *Citizen's Service and Children's Panel Membership.* Children's Panel Chairman's Group: Edinburgh: SWSG, The Scottish Office.

Martin. F, Fox, S, & Murray, K. (1981). *Children Out of Court.* Edinburgh: Scottish Academic Press.

Sloan v B (1991). *Sloan v B and others.* Reported in Scots Law Times, 1991

Social Work (Scotland) Act (1968) (as amended).

CHAPTER 9

SCOTTISH CHILDREN'S HEARINGS AND REPRESENTATION FOR THE CHILD

Donald N. Duquette

INTRODUCTION

My task here is to present briefly some views on the Children's Hearing from an outsider or international perspective. As an admirer of the system, I feel it the height of bad manners to say anything critical or negative. I feel like the person invited to a fine dinner who complains about the soup and argues with the hostess about her choice of wine. Nonetheless, I offer this critique for what it is worth -- to be taken in the constructive and positive spirit in which it is intended.

As I was thinking about points that I wish to make regarding the Children's Hearings, I found one unifying theme, one positive proposal for change -- which incorporates and addresses most of my other concerns. I will, therefore, organise my remarks around one major proposal:

I suggest that children and youth be independently represented in the Children's Hearing. I suggest the introduction of a child advocate who would look out for the interests and wishes of the youth who is the subject of the hearing.

It also follows that parents should enjoy representation in care and protection cases.

This change could strengthen the Children's Hearing in several other ways as well. Let me address some preliminary issues first.

CHARACTERISTICS OF THE ROLE

COOPERATION RATHER THAN CONFRONTATION.

Scotland prides itself, as it should, on a children's justice system which emphasises cooperation rather than confrontation. The underlying goal of the hearing system -- to achieve justice for youth through a cooperative process rather than the confronting, adversarial due process approach -- should be preserved and, in fact, emulated in other countries, particularly at the dispositional stage. The presence of an advocate for the child need not defeat this traditional characteristic of the panels. Because of the unique nonadversarial traditions of the Scottish system, Scotland has an opportunity to establish a child advocate role without importing some of the unwelcome characteristics of an adversarial due process model.

TRAIN ADVOCATES IN COOPERATIVE AND NON-ADVERSARIAL PROBLEM SOLVING TECHNIQUES.

Whoever these advocates turn out to be, train them in cooperative and non-adversarial problem-solving techniques. "Due process" can have a more sensitive and humane tone than the stereotypical view which often conjures up the extreme, e.g. a criminal trial for a capital offence. Participants in the process can be trained in cooperative and problem-solving approaches to the problems of youth and families. An adversarial tone would be discouraged so that an ethic of cooperation is fostered. In fact one responsibility of the child advocate should be to foster cooperative and even consensual resolution. Maintaining this ethic of nonadversarial cooperation as much as possible is essential to preserve the integrity and essential nature of the hearing system. Perhaps mediation techniques could be used within the hearing structure though with representation for parents and the child. (Along the lines suggested by Judge Frank Orlando in his workshop at the Glasgow conference).

Nonetheless, the child advocate - or Office of the Child Advocate - should be able to challenge the recommendations of the local authority when appropriate and raise questions with higher authority if the hearing is not conducted according to the rules.

WHAT SHOULD BE THE ROLE OF THE CHILD ADVOCATE?

The role of the child advocate for the Scottish Hearings would be unique to Scotland. It would borrow concepts and practices from other countries - but would adapt them to the special traditions of the Kilbrandon philosophy and the 21 years experience of the hearing system.

My central goal is to present reasons WHY a child advocate should be introduced into the hearing system and how such a scheme would assist the system. I will not be so bold to attempt to lay out the details of the advocate's role - that is for another day. Here are some of the central elements of the advocate's role, however. The Scottish child advocate role should be:

1) continuous,
2) consistent,
3) independent and,
4) providing universal advocacy on behalf of the child's needs and interests.

These characteristics would distinguish a Scottish child advocate from the current safeguarder role, the guardian ad litem in England and Wales and the U.S. lawyer-based system. <u>Continuous</u> means that the child is appointed an advocate at the very beginning of the process and that advocate serves until the state jurisdiction over the youngster is ended. <u>Consistent</u> means that, to the extent possible, the same advocate would act for the youngster from beginning to end so that the child experiences stability and consistency in that aspect of his or her life, thus modelling the kind of stability and continuity expected of the state agency and the family. <u>Independent</u> means that the child advocate is selected, trained and supervised by an administrative structure separate from the parents, local authority, the hearing panel or the local courts. <u>Universal</u> means that the advocacy system would reach all children who come before the children's hearing (and the court) for care and protection or offence grounds rather than on a selective basis according to some determinants of need.

Once assigned, the advocate would be expected to talk with the youngster, identify his or her interests, and pursue those interests in several venues. The advocate would pursue the child's interests in the formal procedures by representing the child at the children's hearing (and in Sheriff Court if proofs are required). In addition, the advocate would pursue the child's interests <u>outside</u> the hearing - before and after scheduled hearings - with the local authority, the police, the education system, - and perhaps on appeal if necessary. The advocate would act as a sort of "guardian angel" for children facing state intervention.

REPRESENTATION BY WHOM?

WHO should fulfil this broad child advocate function? What type of person with what training should represent the child? This question also should be addressed separately and in more detail than is possible here I am not convinced, however, that lawyers are clearly the only persons able to provide adequate representation - although the advocates used should be trained and have access to lawyers. In fact, lawyers alone would likely import adversarial traditions inconsistent with the hearing system traditions.

England and Wales use experienced social workers as guardians ad litem for the child who then team with solicitors to act for the child. Some American jurisdictions use lay (non lawyer) volunteers - usually matched up with a lawyer. These CASA (Court Appointed Special Advocates) programmes are on the rise in the States. Currently there are about 20,000 CASAs in programmes scattered throughout all 50 states. Some of these offices combine volunteers, social workers and lawyers in a single child advocacy enterprise. It is this latter structure which most appeals to me.

Unlike the Official Solicitor in England and Wales and unlike ombudsman schemes of other countries, the child advocacy scheme I envision would be <u>universal</u>, i.e. reach all children coming before the hearing.

So this is a summary of WHAT I make bold to propose. Let me resist discussing the details of the role of the advocate any further and turn instead to WHY such a role should be created and introduced into the Scottish system. The hearings themselves could be improved in several respects - but modifications should preserve the essential nature of the current system.

WHY A CHILD ADVOCATE FOR THE CHILDREN'S HEARING?

There are a number of weaknesses within the hearing system that the presence of advocates for the youngster (and parents in care and protection cases) could address. I will present four advantages of a child advocacy scheme.

RIGHTS PROTECTION ENHANCED

Rights protection and fairness could be improved in the hearing system while neither losing the focus on the best interests of the child nor sacrificing a cooperative and non adversarial tone as the NORM. (There will almost always be some cases, e.g. where criminal charges are pending, where the cooperative ideal will not be realised.) The presence of a knowledgeable advocate, backed up by an organised office, would help ensure compliance with required procedures and in that way promote fairness. The advocate would strengthen the accountability of the current process. Concerns about shortcomings or violations in a particular case could be raised in the hearing as appropriate, with the reporter, perhaps, or on appeal. Concerns could also be addressed to the social work department, the education department, the police the medical community - whoever has a responsibility for addressing a particular child's needs.

In the first instance the tone of the advocate's actions would be conciliatory - not adversarial. Reasonable people may disagree, however, and the advocate or the child advocacy office should be prepared to bring formal appeal or review actions when warranted.

It would seem likely that the presence of a knowledgeable advocate would be preventive . That is, simply because the advocate is there, the hearing would be less likely to make procedural errors or be overly informal. The presence of the advocate would itself lead to a heightened awareness of the need to follow the rules so that similarly situated parents and children coming before panels can be assured of being treated similarly.

GIVE VOICE TO THE CHILD

As a matter of principle the voice of the child should be heard in proceedings which may affect his or her liberty and future (UN Convention ss 12 and 37(d). The participatory rights of the child, set out in the UN Convention, have been explored in earlier chapters.

The UN Convention provides that a child deprived of his or her liberty shall have prompt access to legal and other appropriate assistance. I am aware that the United Kingdom in its ratification of the Convention reserved the right to continue the Scottish hearing system where legal representation is not permitted. Nonetheless, the convention speaks to an international view that values the child's voice as amplified by independent representation.

Put yourself in the shoes of a child coming before a children's panel. A youngster meeting with three strangers (the panel), a reporter, a social worker AND his parents will be inhibited from speaking freely - even if he or she is reasonably articulate and understands the benevolent intentions of the hearing panel. I have heard of the difficulty of getting a child to express his or her view directly in the hearing. An advocate, meeting with the child in advance, can coax the voice out in private, determine the child's wishes and needs and amplify the child's view in conversation with the social workers and then with the hearing panel.

An advocate would explain the process and LISTEN to the child. The advocate for the child can inform the youngster of what the process involves at every stage; what is to happen, and what will be expected of him or her. An advocate would also listen to the child. A youngster's wishes are not always clear initially. The advocate can help clarify the child's thinking. What would you like to see happen? What are your concerns? What do you want the panel to know? What do you want to tell them? Can I tell them anything for you?

Who would decide what the child's interests are. That is, who would decide the goals of the child advocate? The youngster? The advocate - based on his/her view of the best interests of the child? This is a very complicated question that I cannot do justice to here. But, consistent with Section 12 of the UN Convention, the weight given to the child's views should vary according to the age and maturity of the child. In England and Wales, the social worker guardian ad litem decides what is in the best interests of the child and so instructs a solicitor, also acting on the child's behalf. If, however, the solicitor determines that there is a conflict between this and what the child wishes (i.e. what the child thinks his/her interests are) AND also the child is considered, by the solicitor, mature and intelligent enough, the solicitor takes instruction directly from the child.

Attorneys in the United States are quite muddled about this issue. Most would advocate for the best interests of the child as the attorney sees it, even though the youngster may disagree. The attorney may inform the court of the child's preferences even while advocating for a different view.

I would recommend a presumption at a certain age, say 12 or 14, that the child's wishes determine the advocate's position unless the child is mentally ill or mentally handicapped.

This previous discussion brings home the representational nature of the child advocate. For the older child, it would not be a best interests (or substituted judgement) role. The advocate would attempt to be the <u>voice</u> of the child. As an incidental efficiency, for younger children the representational role of the advocate -- with power to accept grounds for referral on the child's behalf - could reduce the number of cases going to the Sheriff for proof.

COMPLICATED DISPOSITIONAL QUESTIONS

Is a panel of lay volunteers competent to address complicated dispositional questions? A youngster may be seriously emotionally disturbed, present psychiatric problems or drug abuse issues. A panel may face questions of what to do with and for a chronic adolescent sexual offender or a victim of sexual abuse. Of course the panel is guided by the recommendations of the local authority, but to fulfil their function and to act as other than a rubber stamp, they need to understand independently he issues and the options available to them.

An independent evaluation of a case is made more difficult for the panel, however, when there is no independent voice to review and perhaps question the state's proposals. The local authority position comes with the full authority of a large organisation, presumed expert in these family matters. An advocate for the youngster or parents can assist the panel in this regard by assessing the problems independently, arranging for and reviewing professional evaluations when needed, and in other ways clarifying and sharpening the deliberative process. The advocate can assist the panel in understanding the fullness of the young person's needs or the needs of the family.

REGULAR REVIEW PROCESS/MONITORING

One shortcoming of the current hearing system is the absence of regular independent review of compulsory measures of care in under one year according to some established protocol and criteria. Administrative reviews may be useful but lack a certain independence. I understand that reviews before the hearing panel can be requested but this is not done on a regular basis. The parents and the state should be asked to account for their activities. Sometimes the state's plans for a youngster or his family will not be implemented as proposed - despite the best intentions. Legal systems in some other countries, provide for judicial review of the "treatment plan" for the family or the youngster as a check on the performance of the youngster AND the state agencies. These reviews are held as often as every 91 days at a minimum in some jurisdictions.

An advocate for the child can be especially helpful during the treatment phases of the state intervention when welfare of the child is the major focus. There are many interests of the child that the busy local authority may overlook. Once the hearing has decided on compulsory measures of care, the advocate can independently follow up on the effectiveness of these measures. Are they implemented properly? On time? Are they effective? Should the matter be brought back to a hearing?

I can hear someone thinking: Why not ask other participants in the process to perform these child advocacy functions? Adding this role will cost money. It will introduce other participants into the process and complicate it.

However, current provisions for representation and for safeguarders are inadequate to the task. Current representatives are not necessarily trained in advocacy but are more likely to be family members and other support persons. The scope of current representation is too narrow to meet the broad advocacy needs of children and youth as is the current safeguarder role. An entirely new role signals a fresh start free from old traditions.

The breadth and scope of child representation envisioned is not consistent with the roles and responsibilities of the reporter either. To my knowledge there is no counterpart to the reporter in other legal systems (see introduction in chapter 8). The role is unique. The role is valuable. The reporter will certainly be child centred. The child advocate role, however, requires independence and is, therefore, incompatible with the other duties of the reporter.

Similarly, the panel members, committed, gifted and child-centered though they may be, are not continuous or independent enough to fulfil the broad child advocate role.

SUMMARY

Thus I suggest a fundamental change in the Children's Hearing to reflect the greater international awareness of the rights of children. I urge that children and youth be independently represented in those proceedings. Independent representation of children and youth could also help improve the panel's ability to cope with more difficult cases and monitor the state's intervention. For other reasons, parents in child protection proceedings should also have an advocate.

If the decision is taken to adopt an advocacy scheme for youngsters, then a whole other set of issues needs to be confronted. Who should fulfil that role? Lawyers? Perhaps, but not necessarily. Other options are: social workers; a combination of social worker and lawyer, as in England and Wales; a trained volunteer with access to good supervision and to lawyers, as in the US CASA programmes. I personally favour an office based on volunteer advocates with professional support from social workers and lawyers. How should such a scheme be organised and structured to achieve its independence and effectiveness?

CONCLUSION

Injection of advocates for children and parents into the Children's Hearing need not destroy the important welfare philosophy of the Kilbrandon Committee. It is that nurturing focus on the child's welfare which sets this system apart. An advocacy component could merely broaden and improve the reach of the famous welfare focus of the Scottish Children's Hearing.

COMMENTARY BY ANDREW LOCKYER ON DONALD DUQUETTE'S PROPOSAL

This is a response to Donald Duquette's proposal of introducing Child Advocates into the hearings system, necessarily briefer than the idea merits.

Duquette argues for having an "independent representative" who will "look out for the interests and wishes" of children in the hearings system. He mentions the standards of the UN Convention as underscoring the principle of the "child's own voice being heard", and also the right to "prompt access to legal and other assistance". His proposal depends on these ideas being mutually supportive. He notes the UK reservation, to continue the hearings system "where legal representation is not permitted", but reminds us that the convention provides international standards which ought to carry moral weight for us.

CURRENT POSITION: "REPRESENTATIVES" AND "SAFEGUARDERS"

It might be helpful to set out first what arrangements currently exist for representing the child in the hearings system. The rules allow a child or parent to be "accompanied at the hearing" by a "representative":

> "Any person attending any children's hearing for the purpose of representing a child or his parent or both a child and his parent, as the case may be, shall assist the person whom he represents in the discussion of the case of the child with the children's hearing." (Hearing Rule 11(2))

The rules do not exclude lawyers from being representatives, but they are not allowed to "represent" clients, in the sense of being agents speaking for them. A child's representative could not be a substitute for the child's own voice being heard and their views being directly sought. It should be noticed also that the rule is drafted to fit the non-adversarial or consensual model. Representation does not presume "taking sides": the representative can be (and normally is) shared by the family members. This has dangers as well as attractions.

In practice it is commonly a family friend or neighbour who fulfils this role. No legal aid is available for hearings, so if lawyers do attend it is when parents have private means or are the subject of other proceedings for which legal aid is available. When solicitors come to hearings they clearly represent a parent, or parents, but not also the children In these circumstances the child may well be disadvantaged and in need of their own independent support.

HEARING CHAIRMEN HAVE THE OPTION TO APPOINT SAFEGUARDERS

> "..for the purpose of safe-guarding the interests of the child in the proceedings, because there is or may be a conflict, on any matter relevant to the proceedings, between the interests of the child and those of his parent...." (ACT 34A (1)(c)(i))

Sheriffs have the same option, but they may also appoint a legal agent for the child, or a **curator ad litem**, from public funds.

It must be said that children are seldom separately "represented" at hearings and safeguarders are appointed in fewer than 1% of cases. Therefore, at normal hearings reporters, social workers, parents and panel members must either be capable of giving adequate assistance to the child to ensure a fair hearing, or else Duquette's proposal must be accepted.

COSTS AND BENEFITS OF DUQUETTE'S PROPOSAL

My view is that there are costs as well as benefits to the proposal for child advocates. In some circumstances the costs will outweigh the benefits, in others the benefits will outweigh the costs.

The greatest cost of separate advocacy is that it detracts from the consensual model of the hearing. This is **not** because I believe that the representatives will necessarily be adversarial. (I agree this is a danger which could be guarded against by selection and training.) Rather the presumption of the need for separate advocacy, **presupposes a divided family**, where neither parent (nor social worker, nor substitute carer) can adequately support a child in and beyond the hearing. My experience leads me to think that this is not so in most cases.

In general, the best advocate for a child is firstly a parent and secondly a social worker. Significantly, a children's hearing is an arena where an essential function of parenting can be demonstrated; that is, parents standing up for ("representing") their children. It must remain a setting where the direct thoughts and feelings of ordinary people are expressed, without always needing to be "mediated" or "formalised" by official parties.

There are other costs or dangers in introducing additional adults into the hearings' process. It would increase the tendency to make the proceedings a more adult dominated discussion. Also, it would add to the ranks of those who already have a duty to take care of a child's interests: yet another party with a right to intervene. However, these costs are not as important as the effect of demoting parents from an essential parental role.

The costs identified here are neither universal nor indefeasible. There are cases where the parents (or their representatives) cannot be relied upon to assist children, either in putting their points of view or taking care of their interests. There are cases where hearings cannot be confident that the child's point of view is being clearly expressed, and that his or her interest is adequately represented by anyone, including the local authority. The "continuous" role of ensuring that the local authority is carrying out an agreed plan, has special attractions, in certain types of cases.

The potential benefits to children go beyond what is currently provided by existing arrangements. The powers needed would be beyond those of safeguarders and representatives at present. In short, I think the role identified by Donald Duquette is a valuable addition to our means of promoting children's rights and interests **in some cases.** These include those "hard cases" which the Directors of Social Work take to be typical of child protection (see Chapter 8).

I would argue for the role of "child advocacy" to be selective rather than universal, because I do not think it is needed in all or even most cases. But how are cases to be singled out? I favour it being discretionary rather than according to rigid referral criteria. This is because a child's need for additional assistance (like his or her other needs) does not neatly correspond to any formal case characteristics. Children must have the right to an "advocate" if they want one. However, the hearing or sheriff should also have the power to allocate one, when either deem it necessary or desirable, as they do with safeguarders.

The new role would combine and extend those currently fulfilled by safeguarders and representatives. I would endorse most of the powers and duties specified in the Child Advocacy model. In my view the Safeguarder legislation needs to be reformed, and it could without difficulty be extended to embrace the role of "advocate". I would want to avoid the term "advocate" itself, because it derives from an adversarial legal tradition, which presumes a forum in which ordinary people cannot speak for themselves.

RESPONSE TO ANDREW LOCKYER'S COMMENTARY

In response to Andrew Lockyer's comments I make three additional points:

Andrew suggests that if expanded child representation is deemed desirable or necessary, the function could be fulfilled by safeguarders under a broader role definition. While that is a reasonable option, I suggest a different course.

Certainly a broader child advocacy role would be desirable. The advocate should be active in hearings but also outside of hearings and court proceedings, by pursuing the child's interests informally with the local authority etc. Sheriff Brian Kearney has also suggested that it is almost as if we need a whole new role. That is what I believe. The safeguarder role as currently defined in Scottish law is far more restrictive than the child advocate proposed here and would have to be radically redefined. Besides not being defined as broadly as desirable, the safeguarder is not continuous nor universally available. There is a risk, however, that a redefinition of safeguarder, while still using the same name, will be insufficient to break down traditional limitations. Old habits may continue. A new advocate role with a new name clearly communicates and symbolises a new dimension to the hearing system and another Scottish innovation.

Andrew suggests that an appointment of a child advocate perhaps could be done as needed, rather than being universally available. There are some difficulties with a selective approach to advocacy. Who will decide who needs an advocate and on what basis will that decision be made? One youngster may need an advocate more at one stage of the proceedings than another. Should the parents decide? They may have a conflict of interest and may not be truly objective. Should the reporter decide? Deciding whether to appoint an advocate may require looking into the details of the matter and maybe even pre-judging the case. The reporter, with budgetary responsibility, will realise that every time an advocate is appointed, limited funds are eroded by a few more pounds. What criteria for appointment of a child advocate on a selective basis would guarantee that children are provided assistance on an equal basis? The UN convention speaks to "every child deprived of his or her liberty" having access to legal and other appropriate assistance.

Budgetary concerns can be eased by drawing upon the strong volunteer traditions of Scotland and allowing trained and supervised volunteer advocates to fulfil this role -- in all cases.

Andrew cautions, wisely, that we should not lose the child in a more complicated procedure. He warns that it may become easy to have adult talk with adult in proceedings -- thus leaving the child out of the conversation. I agree with this concern. The point, for all but the very youngest child, is to amplify the child's voice and the child's interests. Andrew's concern can and should be addressed by training and clear role definition. The advocate should be a facilitator to get the child's voice heard. Perhaps the advocate could encourage the child to speak directly. In any event the goal for the older child would be to amplify the child's voice, not substitute for it. The child advocate would be more analogous to the use of a microphone, than a tape recorder.

CHAPTER 10

JUSTICE FOR CHILDREN - A STORY WITHOUT AN ENDING

Malcolm Hill and Stewart Asquith

INTRODUCTION

In conclusion, we shall draw together some of the common issues which emerge from the chapters in this book. These have approached justice for children from different national, professional and theoretical standpoints. This reflects the diversity of social and economic conditions in which children live their lives. Whilst some issues of justice touch all children, there are others which are particular to children in specific circumstances - because of poverty, involvement in war, engagement in law-breaking activities, separation from parents, and so on.

Yet one recurrent theme in this volume has been the growing universalisation of concern for children, in two respects. Firstly, the various needs of children are interlinked. Some are more urgent, as when there is severe risk from starvation, a sniper's bullet or an adult's thrashing, but children's rights do not end with the right to survival. It is vital to try and establish the conditions which facilitate the full and rounded development of children as participatory members of society. Secondly responses to the injustices which children experience are increasingly seen to be of international rather than simply national or local concern. In part this reflects our common humanity, but it also recognises that many of the causes of disadvantage in childhood, as in adulthood, lie outside the immediate locality. The capacities of parents and communities to care for children is not only influenced by the policies and resources of national governments, but also greatly affected by such factors as the conditions of international trade and aid, employment decisions by multi-national companies, the aftermath of colonialism and military conflict.

THE UN CONVENTION

These two aspects of universality - the interconnection of needs and the internationalisation of responses - are both reflected in the UN Convention on the Rights of the Child, which has been a thread woven into all of the chapters. This has rightly been portrayed as a major breakthrough for children, with most of the world's governments ratifying a document which encapsulates a wide range of rights for children and lends global moral authority to enhancing the status of children. As Hammarberg (Chapter 3) points out, the implications are greater than the signatories probably realised. The Convention enshrines substantial responsibilities by governments as well as parents and kin for the welfare of children and often these will require considerable commitment of resources if they are to be adequately fulfilled. Furthermore Reid (Chapter 1) argues that the pursuit of children's rights can act as a 'wedge' for human rights more generally, a point echoed in Whande's observations that children's prospects are crucially linked to the economic and social position of adults, especially their mothers (Chapter 5).

The Convention is clearly a vital springboard for all those concerned with and about children, but it is in itself not a panacea. It is the beginning of a story which requires other plot ingredients to ensure progress towards a happy ending. Firstly, the rights embodied in the Convention have to be put into practice and made enforceable. Secondly, justice for children consists of more than formal rights.

We know from Somalia, Bosnia and indeed even wealthy countries (Melton, Chapter 2), that in practice some children do not have the rights to life and health let alone to a wider range of social and developmental opportunities. The mechanisms for putting the Convention into effect are vague and the sanctions for governments' failure to comply are weak. They consist of moral opprobrium and unfavourable reports by the monitoring committee (Chapters 1 and 3). Experience suggests that these are inadequate measures to counter regimes which are deficient, uncaring or impoverished. There are no courts to uphold children's rights, except inasfar as governments choose to incorporate them in national law. Children do not have formal rights of redress, appeal or compensation at an international level. Nor is the Convention accompanied by material assistance which poor countries need if they are to fulfil some of the Articles which require significant resource allocations (e.g. to health and education).

At the national level, in some countries organisations and individuals have been given or have assumed responsibility for safeguarding and furthering children's rights, although often their power and influence is quite circumscribed. Even before the UN Convention was signed, there had been a trend to establish posts such as Children's Rights Officers or Commissioners. They operate as watchdogs and advocates in relation to central and local government departments. Many of these were modelled on the Scandinavian innovation of Ombudsman (Barneombud) (Melton, Chapter 2; Flekkoy, 1989). In addition, responsibility for implementing the Convention, disseminating its contents and coordinating the actions of agencies involved with children, has usually been given to a branch of government or an arms-length Committee. For instance, in Canada the Children's Bureau in Ottawa was given this remit, whilst in Vietnam the work is done by the Committee for the Protection, Care and Education of Children, which is directly accountable to the council of ministers (O.S.E.D.C., 1992). It is very easy for ministries or councils concerned with children or family matters to be sidelined (Craven et al., 1982). Hammarberg suggests that children's rights must be seen as a central political issue if they are not to be marginalised (Chapter 3). It is also essential that they do not remain paper rights, but are backed up by corresponding attitudes, services and resources.

RIGHTS AND JUSTICE

It is clear that legislation is necessary but not sufficient to secure justice for children, whether that is conceptualised in terms of rights, needs, fairness or equality. Goonesekere (Chapter 4) argues that for children to achieve justice they need not only civil rights but socio-economic or welfare rights. This in turn means that countries need effective economic and social systems so that children are not exploited or placed at a disadvantage. Social justice requires that children have not only entitlements (e.g. to education) but the capacity to use them (Plant, 1992).

The roots of child labour, trafficking and separation often lie in poverty. Street children in Latin America and elsewhere are often not abandoned, but contributing to a precarious family economy either directly through their earnings or by fending for themselves for lengthy periods in order to reduce costs for their parents (Glauser, 1990, Penna Firme, Chapter 6)). In India and elsewhere poverty leads many children to work in crafts and industries. Employers benefit from the cheap labour and the parents cannot afford to keep their children at school (Burra, 1990). The products of child labour and sometimes children's own bodies are sold to Western consumers and tourists, so that an international dimension helps sustain this problem. A combination of government legislation and resources is necessary to tackle such problems in the home country, but financial assistance and cessation of demand may be needed from abroad as well (Ennew, 1986; Doek, 1991). The World Summit for Children gave impetus to concerted action, particularly in relation to the health and educational needs of children. There have been significant advances in the last decade, such as the dramatic increase in immunisation coverage, but much remains to be done to reduce malnutrition and life-threatening diseases in childhood (Grant, 1991).

In a different context - that of post-Communist Eastern Europe - Triseliotis (Chapter 7) notes that significant improvements in the lives of children currently in residential institutions requires the development of preventive measures and alternative systems of public care. This involves the creation of a welfare infrastructure as well as legal and political changes. Both universal and specialist policy elements are necessary. Adequate income maintenance programmes are needed to enable families to look after their own children, whilst a professional social work service is vital to improve substitute care arrangements. The latter includes the promotion of foster care for young children and small scale specialist residential care for older children to replace large institutions, as has happened in much of Western Europe, though it must be remembered that even there the shift to more personalised forms of substitute care is quite recent (Gottesman, 1991).

The need for such an approach is not confined to Romania. Large impersonal institutions with little individualised care are common not only in Eastern Europe (Melton, Chapter 2) but also in many other parts of the world. Even in relatively prosperous Hong Kong, a prominent indigenous child welfare organisation which has developed family group homes, still runs a large establishment with rows of closely spaced cots for infants and dormitories for 30 children. The only pictures which adorn the walls are of benefactors rather than the children living there.

As well as top-down initiatives by governments, bottom-up community development strategies can assist families and children. Collective action is often more in keeping with traditional cultures than individualistic policies (Castillo-Rios, 1990). According to Penna Firme (Chapter 6), the success of new legislation for children and adolescents in Brazil depends on the involvement of young people themselves in social movements which support a community spirit. Young people with deviant life-styles can be reconnected to mainstream society by measures which respect and respond to their own values and interests. Melton (Chapter 2) argues that the absence of grass-roots organisations for children was weakened the position of children in Norway despite its well-established Ombudsman.

For refugees and children affected by war or hunger, local resources may be inadequate or totally lacking and Whande makes a passionate appeal for help from richer countries (Chapter 5). Ideally this should be provided in ways which do not undermine the power, status and dignity of families in need. It should sustain and promote individual and collective self-help initiatives rather than threaten them.

There is, of course, already a considerable amount of financial, material and advisory aid. For instance, the European Community sends emergency and food aid, particularly to sub-Saharan Africa (Commission of the EC, 1991). However, the effectiveness of aid programmes and their sensitivity to the local environment and economy have been questioned. International assistance can promote community development, as with Afghan refugee families in Pakistan (Bartle and Segerstrom, 1992). But external aid can also undermine rather than support community-based approaches, e.g. by setting up separate villages for war orphans in Mozambique, rather than providing relief so that local families can care for them (Kanji, 1990).

JUSTICE AND WELFARE

In addition to children suffering from physical hardship, governments normally take some responsibility for two other significant groups of children - those whose development is impaired by family circumstances and young people who commit offences. Sometimes referred to as 'troubled' and 'troublesome' children respectively, these groupings overlap and both tend to come from disadvantaged backgrounds. Particularly in the 1960's and 1970's there was a trend towards dealing in a similar fashion with all children in difficulty who were thought to require compulsory intervention, but this was followed by a reversion in some jurisdictions to sharper demarcation.

With regard to compulsory intervention by the state to deal with children's lawbreaking, it has been customary to distinguish two types of system. According to this model, the 'justice' system is based on due process and sentencing proportional to the 'crime', whilst the 'welfare' system is characterised by greater informality and disposals intended to meet the needs of the young person. The 'welfare' approach lends itself more readily to the integration of judicial and service responses to both juvenile offending and child protection. In reality, there has been considerable overlap in assumptions and practices (King, 1981), so that it is preferable to think of differences in emphasis rather than a total opposition.

The term 'justice' in this context is being used in a legal sense embracing safeguards for individual liberty and against arbitrary treatment. That contrasts with the wider concept of social justice which has been used in this book to denote minimum standards for children beyond basic subsistence and the minimisation of unfairnesses between children as regards social and economic opportunities. It is a matter of debate whether a 'justice' model, 'welfare' model or some combination of the two best serves the aim of improving social justice for children. Indeed given the variety of circumstances affecting troubled and troublesome children, any particular system is likely to do well by some, but not others - hopefully a small minority in most cases.

During the 1980's, several countries including Canada, New Zealand and England & Wales moved to separate treatment of offenders from treatment of other children and generally shifted towards a more 'justice' oriented model for the former (Ball, 1990; Doolan, 1990; Leschied et al., 1991). Part of the reason for this was that the welfare model was thought to reduce young people's ability to assert their innocence and to encourage indeterminate 'sentences' on the basis of professional judgements (Geach and Szwed, 1983). Scotland bucked this trend and has adhered to the principle that the child's welfare should be the primary consideration, irrespective of the reason for public concern. Proponents of the system cite evidence that children's rights can be sustained by a combination of informal processes and formal procedures outside a court setting (Lockyer, Chapter 8; Martin and Murray, 1982).

CHILDREN, PARENTS AND THE STATE

Children's initial dependence on their parents (or other carers) means that these adults have a crucial interest in their welfare. In virtually all cultures children have a special value and parents are expected to have a major role in looking after them, although the aims and manner of childrearing have varied enormously. The parent-child relationship has commonly been regarded in terms of parents' rights and parental authority as much as children's entitlements. Often emphasis is given to children's duties towards parents and the senior generation in general, as in Islamic teachings. Ahmad (1990) observes that most black communities evaluate self-development and self-achievements 'against the fulfilment of self-responsibility of the individual towards his or her family and community' (p. 14). Commonly, child-rearing has been viewed as promoting family identity and loyalty (Dixon, 1985; Chow, 1987) rather than individual self-actualisation as in modern Western societies. Western writers also regard some form of parental authority as vital to enable parents to carry out daily care and to enable children to learn about and negotiate limits to freedom (Freeman, 1983; Elshtain, 1991). However it is being increasingly recognised that parental rights are derived from and dependent on the fulfilment of responsibilities towards children (Newell, 1991). When the State through its officials or professionals has misgivings about the quality of parenting in a particular family then complex triangular conflicts of interests and rights may arise from the differing viewpoints of child, parent and State.

The UN Convention makes it clear that it is the primary responsibility of parents to secure the rights and welfare of their children. Yet it also affirms that states have a responsibility to intervene when parents are unable or unwilling to afford proper care. This illustrates how the Convention contains broad principles which may be laudable in themselves, but may conflict in particular instances. It is by no means straightforward to determine how such conflicts are to be resolved in practice. The law cannot prescribe responses to every particular circumstance, so that outcomes will depend on discretionary decision-making by family members, officials, professionals and the judiciary. This can result in actions which are responsive to individual family situations, but also runs the risk of arbitrariness and 'expert' domination (Adler and Asquith, 1981). Judgements about acceptable standards of parenting are notoriously difficult and the intervention of public bodies to override parental rights should be subject to judicial review and appeal (Hill et al., 1992).

In many instances it will be possible to gain agreement even when parties are initially opposed. For instance there is a growing trend to settle disputes about divorce and access through mediation rather than adversarial battles in court. Such mediation has a long tradition in China, for instance. In relation to both child protection and dealing with juvenile offending, Lockyer (Chapter 8) argues that the Scottish Children's Hearings System offers a consensual alternative to more formal and legalistic youth or family court systems. Duquette (Chapter 9) also recognises the value of non-adversarial approaches, but believes they can be strengthened by the incorporation of due process and the continuous availability to a child of an independent advocate.

There is also potential conflict between Article 3 of the Convention, which asserts that the best interests of the child shall be a primary consideration in actions concerning children, and Article 12, which requires that the child's views should be heard. It is not uncommon for children to want things which one or more adults believe are not in their interests. If children's views are not simply to be heard but then ignored, questions arise about how much weight should be given to their wishes and in what circumstances these might outweigh adult perceptions. The very notion of 'best interests' has been much contested and has been portrayed by some as a rationale for professional or state control of children (Geach and Szwed, 1983). However, most people would probably agree that a balance is needed amongst the different positions which emphasise protectionist, parentalist and liberationist concerns (Adler, 1985).

Ensuring that children have an effective voice, particularly when their liberty is at stake, can be problematic. When given the right to speak, children can easily be inhibited by formality, the presence of strangers and a generally adult-centred meeting. They may also be ignorant of their procedural rights (Barford and Wattam, 1991; Batty and Robson, 1992; Smith, 1991). Duquette and Lockyer debate this issue in relation to the Scottish Hearings System (Chapters 8 and 9) although the principles are applicable to other settings such as courts, case conferences or school reviews. Duquette believes that universal access to an advocate is essential to ensure that, in an adult forum, children's views can be properly represented with full awareness of legal rights and implications. Lockyer counters that children usually already have trusted people who can represent them (notably parents or other relatives) and that professional or lay members of the existing system ought to be able to safeguard the child's rights without recourse to an outsider in most cases.

The UN Convention is mainly concerned with protective and social rights rather than with freedoms for self-determination and political rights (e.g. to vote, make sexual choices) as advocated by child liberationists (Franklin, 1986). Whilst the Convention accords participatory rights to children in relation to their 'age and maturity', some commentators have gone further and argued that there should be a separate intermediate status for teenagers which recognises their emerging competence and responsibility (Lindley, 1991). It is held that can make informed choices and so should have greater autonomy. Certainly there is a stronger case on physical and cognitive grounds for extending certain adult rights to teenagers than to younger children. However, even the limited recognition in the Convention of the child's role in decision-making was more controversial and harder to gain support for than rights to protection and social provision, since the former is more threatening to the adult and often patriarchal authority which is present to differing degrees in virtually all societies (Reid, Chapter 1).

RIGHTS, DISCRIMINATION AND RELATIVISM

Article 2 of the Convention states that all the other rights contained in the document apply without discrimination of any kind and that children should be protected from discrimination. Article 30 embodies the entitlement of children to their own culture, language and religion. The Convention also worded carefully its provisions on adoption, since Islamic law does not recognise the full transfer of parental authority and inheritance rights to someone else (Van Loon, 1990). There can be a delicate interplay between respect for cultural diversity and ensuring that children are not ill-treated or discriminated against in the name of tradition.

Goonesekere (Chapter 4) makes a powerful case for the application of universal standards across cultures. For instance this means that girls should not be not treated less favourably than males on religious grounds and child abuse cannot be justified as a form of customary chastisement. Triseliotis (Chapter 7) also states that bad practices in residential care should not be condoned, wherever they occur, although it is important to understand their historical and political origins. Goonesekere recommends a 'two-track' model, consisting of a compulsory basic code to apply everywhere together with the option of additional customary laws in local areas. Countries such as New Zealand and the United States have transferred back to indigenous peoples much of the jurisdiction in child welfare matters which was formerly taken away from them (Edwards and Egbert-Edwards, 1989).

When children are thought to be at risk, they should not be left to suffer for fear of imposing 'majority' standards, but intervention should be sensitive to local culture and include local representatives. The dangers of insensitive action are well illustrated by the removal of large numbers of Native American Indian children from their homes and communities on the grounds of neglect and ill-treatment up to the 1970's. Often the result was emotional trauma, cultural disorientation and social isolation (Mackenzie and Hudson, 1985; Bagley, 1991). In Britain, concern has been expressed about 'punitive' predispositions to view black families negatively, but also about the opposite 'liberal' approach of wishing not to make judgements about other cultures which has contributed to failures to protect children from injury and even death (Channor and Parton, 1990; Gambe et al., 1992).

The problem of assisting children in severe difficulty without severing cultural ties is also illustrated by inter-country adoption. When the world became aware of the plight of children in orphanages in Romania (and later Albania and Russia), many childless couples from elsewhere presented themselves as the solution, although as Triseliotis observes far fewer rushed to help starving African children (Chapter 7). The Convention recognises that inter-country adoption may be the best option for some abandoned children. It appears that children adopted from Korea, Latin America and elsewhere in Europe and North America have mostly made good progress after a bleak start in life, although there can be problems of discrimination, social identity and educational achievement (Altstein and Simon, 1991; Thoburn and Charles, 1992). Adoptive parents do often make genuine attempts to keep the children in touch with their countries and cultures of origin, but distance inevitably restricts the scope of this in most cases. Although intercountry adoption undoubtedly helps some children, this should only be a short-term response, since the long-term need is for the material, health and cultural support to be provided so that children can stay with their parents, kin or local foster carers. Nobody now thinks that an appropriate response to childhood urban deprivation in Britain is to ship children thousands of miles overseas, as happened from the 1860's until the 1960's (Wagner, 1982; Bean and Melville, 1989).

The Convention tends to side-step issues of gender discrimination. The use of the term "parents" throughout acknowledges equal legal responsibilities of mothers and fathers. This ignores the fact that in most societies the main task of day to day care of children is carried by women (Whande, Chapter 5) - a role which is usually given low status and limits women's chances to engage fully in more powerful and rewarding public roles. If justice is to mean equal opportunity to participate in favoured social activities, then fundamental changes in attitudes and socialisation are essential. UNICEF has promoted initiatives to improve the relative lot of girls, such as assisting with education in Bangladesh and Nepal.

CONCLUSION

Justice for children has now become established as a world-wide issue. The welfare of children is everyone's concern and responsibility. Within nations a co-ordinated strategy is required. Formal rights to protection and for participation should be embodied in the law and be accompanied by the necessary mechanisms and resources to make those rights effective. Equally, recognition should be given to children's welfare rights to the provision of supportive services and adequate income necessary for their full development. International measures are needed too, both to deal with particular problems like child abduction, trafficking and intercountry adoption and to provide resources in ways which are responsive to the needs and wishes of children and their families.

The UN Convention has provided a spur to action. There has been a proliferation of committees, agencies and posts at different levels to put into effect and monitor the Convention. These should help ensure that children's interests are furthered, but there are dangers of adding new systems rather than improving existing systems and processes. It is also important that as far as possible children themselves should be consulted and involved in organisations and arrangements set up to further their rights.

This book has told a story which portrays a new development for children's welfare centred on the international UN Convention, but which remains rooted in the time-honoured concerns of families and local communities for their children. There are now concerted efforts to ensure that all children have good life chances, but for too many children the aspirations we have described remain a fairy-tale.

We hope that a sequel to depict progress in the twenty first century will show that the gap between hope and reality has been much reduced.

REFERENCES

Ahmad, B. (1990) *Black Perspectives on Social Work* Venture Press, Birmingham.

Adler, M. and Asquith, S. (eds.) *Discretion and Welfare* Heinemann, London.

Adler, R. M. (1985) *Taking Juvenile Justice Seriously* Scottish Academic Press, Edinburgh.

Altstein, H. and Simon, R. J. (eds.) (1991) *Intercountry Adoption* Prager, New York.

Bagley, C. (1991) Canada: A Policy Analysis and Research Report', in Altstein, H. and Simon, R. J. (eds.) *Intercountry Adoption* Prager, New York.

Ball, C. (1990) 'The Children Act, 1989: origins, aims and current concerns', in Carter, P., Jeffs, T. and Smith, M. (eds.) *Social Work and Social Welfare*, Open University Press, Milton Keynes.

Barford, R. and Wattam, C. (1991) 'Children's participation in decision-making', *Practice* 5, 2, 93-102.

Bartle, P. and Segerstrom, E. (1992) 'A community self-help approach', *Children Worldwide* 19, 1, 6-9.

Batty, D. and Robson, J. (eds.) (1992) *Statutory Reviews in Practice* BAAF, London.

Bean, P. and Melville, J. (1989) *Lost Children of the Empire* Unwin Hyman, London.

Burra, N. (1990) 'Child labour in India: An Overview', in J. Ross and V. Bergum (eds.) *Through the Looking Glass: Children and Health Promotion* Canadian Public Health Association, Ottawa.

Castillo-Rios, C. (1990) 'Childhood problems in underdeveloped areas of the Third World' in J. Ross and V. Bergum (eds.) *Through the Looking Glass: Children and Health Promotion* Canadian Public Health Association, Ottawa.

Channor, Y. and Parton, N. (1990) 'Racism, cultural relativisn and child abuse', in Violence Against Children Study Group *Taking Child Abuse Seriously* Unwin Hyman, London.

Chow, N.W.S. (1987) 'Western and Chinese ideas of social welfare', *International Social Work* 30, 31-41.

Commission of the European Community (1991) *The Community and the Third World* Office for Official Publications of the European Communities, Luxembourg.

Craven, E., Rimmer, L. and Wicks, M. (1982) *Family Issues and Public Policy* Study Commission on the Family, London.

Dixon, J. (1985) 'China', in Dixon, J. and Kim, H. S. (eds.) *Social Welfare in Asia* Croom Helm, London.

Doek, J. E. (1991) 'Management of child abuse and neglect at the international level: Trends and Perspectives', *Child Abuse and Neglect* 15, 1, 51-56.

Doolan, M. P. (1990) 'Youth justice reform in New Zealand', *Community Alternatives*, 2, 1, 77-90.

Edwards, E. D. and Egbert-Edwards, M. (1989) 'The American Indian Child Welfare Act: Achievements and Recommendations', in J. Hudson and B. Galaway (eds.) *The State as Parent* Kluwer, Dordrecht

Elshtain, J. B. (1991) 'The family, democratic politics and the question of authority' in Scarre, G. (ed.) *Children, Parents and Politics* Cambridge University Press, Cambridge.

Ennew, J. (1986) *The Sexual Exploitation of Children* Polity Press, Cambridge.

Franklin, B. (ed.) (1986) *The Rights of Children* Blackwell, Oxford.

Freeman, M. D. A. (1983) *The Rights and Wrongs of Children* Pinter, London.

Flekkoy, M. (1989) 'An Ombudsman for Children: The Norwegian experience', *Children Worldwide* 3, 15-17.

Gambe D., Gomes, J., Kapur, V., Rangel, M. and Stubbs, P. (1992) *Improving Practice with Children and Families* CCETSW, London.

Geach, H. and Szwed, E. (1983) *Providing Civil Justice for Children* Edward Arnold, London.

Glauser, B. (1990) 'Street children: Deconstructing a construct', in A. James and A. Prout (eds.) *Constructing and Reconstructing Childhood: Contemporary Issues in the Sociological Study of the Child* Falmer Press, London.

Gottesman, M. (ed.) (1991) *Residential Child Care: An International Reader* Whiting and Birch, London.

Grant, J. P. (1991) *The State of the World's Children* UNICEF/Oxford University Press, Oxford.

Hill, M. Lambert, L., Triseliotis, J. and Buist, M. (1992) 'Making judgements about parenting: The example of freeing for adoption', *British Journal of Social Work* 22, 373-389.

Kanji, N. (1990) 'War and children in Mozambique: Is international aid strengthening or eroding community-based policies?', *Community Development Journal* 25, 2, 102-112.

King, M. (ed.) (1981) *Children, Welfare and Justice* Batsford, London.

Leschied, A. W., Jaffe, P. G. and Willis, W. (1991) *The Young Offenders Act: A Revolution in Canadian Juvenile Justice*, University Of Toronto Press, Toronto.

Lindley, R. (1991) 'Teenagers and other children', in Scarre, G. (ed.) *Children, Parents and Politics* Cambridge University Press, Cambridge.

McKenzie, B. and Hudson, P. (1985) 'Native children, child welfare and the colonization of Native People', in Levitt, K. L. and Wharf, B. (eds.) *The Challenge of Child Welfare* University of British Columbia Press, Vancouver.

Martin, F. M. and Murray, K. (1982) *The Scottish Juvenile Justice System* Scottish Academic Press, Edinburgh.

Newell, P. (1991) *The UN Convention and Children's Rights in the UK* National Children's Bureau, London.

Organisation for the Support and Education of Disadvantaged Children (1992) *Child Right Issues* Su That, Hanoi.

Plant, R. (1992) 'Citizenship, rights and welfare', in Coote, A. (ed.) *The Welfare of Citizens*, IPPR, London.

Smith, R. (1991) 'Child care: Welfare, protection or rights?' *Journal of Social Welfare and Family Law* 469-481.

Thoburn, J. and Charles, M. (1992) *A Review of Research which is Relevant to Intercountry Adoption* Department of Health, London.

Van Loon, J. H. A. (1990) *Report on Intercountry Adoption* Permanent Bureau of the Conference, The Hague.

Wagner, G. (1982) *Children of the Empire* Weidenfeld and Nicholson, London.

INDEX

APPENDIX

The UN Convention on the Rights of the Child

Adopted by the General Assembly of the United Nations on 20 November 1989, and in force since September 2, 1990

Preamble

The States Parties to the present Convention,

Considering that in accordance with the principles proclaimed in the Charter of the United Nations, recognition of the inherent dignity and of the equal and inalienable rights of all members of the human family is the foundation of freedom, justice and peace in the world,

Bearing in mind that the peoples of the United Nations have, in the Charter, reaffirmed their faith in fundamental human rights and in the dignity and worth of the human person, and have determined to promote social progress and better standards of life in larger freedom,

Recognizing that the United Nations has, in the Universal Declaration of Human Rights and in the international Covenants on Human Rights, proclaimed and agreed that everyone is entitled to all the rights and freedoms set forth therein, without distinction of any kind, such as race, colour, sex, language, religion, political or other opinion, national or social origin, property, birth or other status,

Recalling that, in the Universal Declaration of Human Rights, the United Nations has proclaimed that childhood is entitled to special care and assistance,

Convinced that the family, as the fundamental group of society and the natural environment for the growth and well-being of all its members and particularly children, should be afforded the necessary protection and assistance so that it can fully assume its responsibilities within the community.

Recognizing that the child, for the full and harmonious development of his or her personality, should grow up in a family environment, in an atmosphere of happiness, love and understanding,

Considering that the child should be fully prepared to live an individual life in society, and brought up in the spirit of the ideals proclaimed in the Charter of the United Nations, and in particular in the spirit of peace, dignity, tolerance, freedom, equality and solidarity.

Bearing in mind that the need for extending particular care to the child has been stated in the Geneva Declaration on the Rights of the Child of 1924 and in the Declaration of the Rights of the Child adopted by the United Nations in 1959 and recognized in the Universal Declaration of Human Rights, in the International Covenant on Civil and Political Rights (in particular in articles 23 and 24), in the international Covenant on Economic, Social and Cultural Rights (in particular in its article 10) and in the statutes and relevant instruments of specialized agencies and international organizations concerned with the welfare of children,

Bearing in mind that, as indicated in the Declaration of the Rights of the Child adopted by the General Assembly of the United Nations on 20 November 1959, 'the child, by reason of his physical and mental immaturity, needs special safeguards and care, including appropriate legal protection, before as well as after birth,'

Recalling the provisions of the Declaration on Social and Legal Principles relating to the Protection and Welfare of Children. with Special Reference to Foster Placement and Adoption Nationally and Internationally (General Assembly Resolution 41/85 of 3 December 1986); the United Nations Standard Minimum Rules for the Administration of Juvenile Justice ('The Beijing Rules') (General Assembly Resolution 40/33 of 29 November 1985); and the Declaration on the Protection of Women and Children in Emergency and Armed Conflict (General Assembly Resolution 3318 (XXIX) of 14 December 1974),

Recognizing that in all countries in the world there are children living in exceptionally difficult conditions, and that such children need special consideration,

Taking due account of the importance of the traditions and cultural values of each people for the protection and harmonious development of the child,

Recognizing the importance of internal co-operation for improving the living conditions of children in every country, in particular in the developing countries,

Have agreed as follows:

PART I

Article 1: Definition of a child
For the purposes of the present Convention a child means every human being below the age of 18 years unless, under the law applicable to the child, majority is attained earlier.

Article 2: Non-discrimination

1. The States Parties to the present Convention shall respect and ensure the rights set forth in this Convention to each child within their jurisdiction without discrimination of any kind, irrespective of the child's or his or her parents's or legal guardians's race, colour, sex, language, religion, political or other opinion, national, ethnic or social origin, property, disability, birth or other status.

2. States Parties shall take all appropriate measures to ensure that the child is protected against all forms of discrimination or punishment on the basis of the status, activities, expressed opinions, or beliefs of the child's parents, legal guardians, or family members.

Article 3: Best interests of the child

1. In all actions concerning children, whether undertaken by public or private social welfare institutions, courts of law, administrative authorities or legislative bodies, the best interests of the child shall be a primary consideration.

2. States Parties undertake to ensure the child such protection and care as is necessary for his or her well-being, taking into account the rights and duties of his or her parents, legal guardians, or other individuals legally responsible for him or her, and, to this end, shall take all appropriate legislative and administrative measures.

3. States Parties shall ensure that the institutions, services and facilities responsible for the care or protection of children shall conform with the standards established by competent authorities, particularly in the areas of safety, health, in the number and suitability of their staff as well as competent supervision.

Article 4: Implementation of rights

States Parties shall undertake all appropriate legislative, administrative, and other measures, for the implementation of the rights recognized in this Convention. In regard to economic, social and cultural rights, States Parties shall undertake such measures to the maximum extent of their available resources and, where needed, within the framework of international co-operation.

Article 5: Parental guidance and the child's evolving capacities

States Parties shall respect the responsibilities, rights, and duties of parents or, where applicable, the members of the extended family or community as provided for by the local custom, legal guardians or other persons legally responsible for the child, to provide, in a manner consistent with the evolving capacities of the child, appropriate direction and guidance in the exercise by the child of the rights recognized in the present Convention.

Article 6: Survival and development
1. States Parties recognize that every child has the inherent right to life.
2. States Parties shall ensure to the maximum extent possible the survival and development of the child.

Article 7: Name and nationality
1. The child shall be registered immediately after birth and shall have the right from birth to a name, the right to acquire a nationality, and. as far as possible, the right to know and be cared for by his or her parents.
2. States Parties shall ensure the implementation of these rights in accordance with their national law and their obligations under the relevant international instruments in this field, in particular where the child would otherwise be stateless.

Article 8: Preservation of identity
1. States Parties undertake to respect the right of the child to preserve his or her identity, including nationality, name and family relations as recognized by law without unlawful interference.
2. Where a child is illegally deprived of some or all of the elements of his or her identity, States Parties shall provide appropriate assistance and protection, with a view to speedily re-establishing his or her identity.

Article 9: Separation from parents
1. States Parties shall ensure that a child shall not be separated from his or her parents against their will, except when competent authorities subject to judicial review determine, in accordance with applicable law and procedures, that such separation is necessary for the best interests of the child. Such determination may be necessary in a particular case such as one involving abuse or neglect of the child by the parents. or one where the parents are living separately and a decision must be made as to the child's place of residence.
2. In any proceedings pursuant to paragraph 1, all interested parties shall be given an opportunity to participate in the proceedings and make their views known.
3. States Parties shall respect the right of the child who is separated from one or both parents to maintain personal relations and direct contact with both parents on a regular basis, except if it is contrary to the child's best interests.
4. Where such separation result from any action initiated by a State Party, such as the detention, imprisonment, exile, deportation or death (including death arising from any cause while the person is in the custody of the State) of one or both parents or of the child, that State Party shall, upon request, provide the parents, the child or, if appropriate,

another member of the family with the essential information concerning the whereabouts of the absent member(s) of the family unless the provision of the information would be detrimental to the well-being of the child. States Parties shall further ensure that the submission of such a request shall of itself entail no adverse consequences for the person(s) concerned.

Article 10: Family reunification
1. In accordance with the obligations of States Parties under article 9, paragraph 1, applications by a child or his or her parents to enter or leave a State Party for the purpose of family reunification shall be dealt with by States Parties in a positive, humane and expeditious manner. States Parties shall further ensure that the submission of such a request shall entail no adverse consequences for the applicants and for the members of their family.
2. A child whose parents reside in different States shall have the right to maintain on regular basis save in exceptional circumstances personal relations and direct contacts with both parents. Towards that end and in accordance with the obligation of States Parties under article 9, paragraph 2, States Parties shall respect the right of the child and his or her parents to leave any country, including their own, and to enter their own country. The right to leave any country shall be subject only to such restrictions as are prescribed by law and which are necessary to protect the national security, public order (*ordre public*), public health or morals or the rights and freedoms of others and are consistent with the other rights recognized in the present Convention.

Article 11: Illicit transfer and non-return
1. State Party shall take measures to combat the illicit transfer and non-return of children abroad.
2. To this end States Parties shall promote the conclusion of bilateral or multilateral agreements or accession to existing agreements.

Article 12: The child's opinion
1. States Parties shall assure to the child who is capable of forming his or her own views the right to express those views freely in all matters affecting the child, the views of the child being given due weight in accordance with the age and maturity of the child.
2. For this purpose, the child shall in particular be provided the opportunity to be heard in any judicial and administrative proceedings affecting the child, either directly, or through a representative or an appropriate body, in a manner consistent with the procedural rules of national law.

Article 13: Freedom of expression
1. The child shall have the right to freedom of expression: this right shall include freedom to seek, receive and impart information and ideas of all kinds, regardless of frontiers, either orally, in writing or in print, in the form of art, or through any other media of the child's choice.
2. The exercise of this right may be subject to certain restrictions, but these shall only be such as are provided by law and are necessary:
   (a) for respect of the rights or reputations of others; or
   (b) for the protection of national security or of public order (*ordre public*), or of public health or morals.

Article 14: Freedom of thought, conscience and religion
1. States Parties shall respect the right of the child to freedom of thought. conscience and religion.
2. States Parties shall respect the rights and duties of the parents and. when applicable, legal guardians, to provide direction to the child in the exercise of his or her right in a manner consistent with the evolving capacities of the child.
3. Freedom to manifest one's religion or beliefs may be subject only to such limitations as are prescribed by law and are necessary to protect public safety, order, health, or morals or the fundamental rights and freedoms of others.

Article 15: Freedom of association
1. States Parties recognize the rights of the child to freedom of association and to freedom of peaceful assembly.
2. No restrictions may be placed on the exercise of these rights other than those imposed in conformity with the law and which are necessary in a democratic society in the interests of national security or public safety. public order (*ordre public*), the protection of public health or morals or the protection of the rights and freedoms of others.

Article 16: Protection of privacy
1. No child shall be subjected to arbitrary or unlawful interference with his or her privacy, family, home or correspondence. nor to unlawful attacks on his or her honour and reputation.
2. The child has the right to the protection of the law against such interference or attacks.

Article 17: Access to appropriate information
States Parties recognize the important function performed by the mass media and shall ensure that the child has access to information and material from a diversity of national and international sources, especially those aimed at

the promotion of his or her social, spiritual and moral well-being and physical and mental health. To this end, States Parties shall:

(a) Encourage the mass media to disseminate information and material of social and cultural benefit to the child and in accordance with the spirit of article 29;
(b) Encourage international co-operation in the production, exchange and dissemination of such information and material from a diversity of cultural, national and international sources;
(c) Encourage the production and dissemination of children's books;
(d) Encourage the mass media to have particular regard to the linguistic needs of the child who belongs to a minority group or who is indigenous;
(e) Encourage the development of appropriate guidelines for the protection of the child from information and material injurious to his or her well-being bearing in mind the provisions of articles 13 and 18.

Article 18: Parental responsibilities
1. States Parties shall use their best efforts to ensure recognition of the principle that both parents have common responsibilities for the upbringing and development of the child. Parents or, as the case may be, legal guardians. have the primary responsibility for the upbringing and development of the child. The best interest of the child will be their basic concern.
2. For the purpose of guaranteeing and promoting the rights set forth in this Convention. States Parties shall render appropriate assistance to parents and legal guardians in the performance of their child-rearing responsibilities and shall ensure the development of institutions. facilities and services for the care of children.
3. States Parties shall take all appropriate measures to ensure that children of working parents have the right to benefit from child care services and facilities for which they are eligible.

Article 19: Protection from abuse and neglect
1. States Parties shall take all appropriate legislative. administrative. social and educational measures to protect the child from all forms of physical or mental violence. injury or abuse, neglect or negligent treatment, maltreatment or exploitation including sexual abuse, while in the care of parent(s), legal guardian(s) or any other person who has the care of the child.
2. Such protective measures should, as appropriate. include effective procedures for the establishment of social programmes to provide necessary support for the child and for those who have the care of the child, as well as for other forms of prevention and for identification, reporting,

referral, investigation, treatment, and follow-up of instances of child maltreatment described heretofore, and, as appropriate. for judicial involvement.

Article 20: Protection of children without families
1. A child temporarily or permanently deprived of his or her family environment, or in whose own best interests cannot be allowed to remain in that environment, shall be entitled to special protection and assistance provided by the State.
2. States Parties shall in accordance with their national laws ensure alternative care for such a child.
3. Such care could include. *inter alia*, foster placement. Kafala of Islamic law, adoption, or if necessary placement in suitable institutions for the care of children. When considering solutions, due regard shall be paid to the desirability of continuity in a child's upbringing and to the child's ethnic, religious, cultural and linguistic background.

Article 21: Adoption
States Parties which recognize and/or permit the system of adoption shall ensure that the best interests of the child shall be the paramount consideration and they shall:
  (a) ensure that the adoption of a child is authorized only by competent authorities who determine. in accordance with applicable law and procedures and on the basis of all pertinent and reliable information. that the adoption is permissible in view of the child's status concerning parents, relatives and legal guardians and that, if required. the persons concerned have given their informed consent to the adoption on the basis of such counselling as may be necessary;
  (b) recognize that intercountry adoption may be considered as an alternative means of child's care. if the child cannot be placed in a foster or an adoptive family or cannot in any suitable manner be cared for in the child's country of origin;
  (c) ensure that the child concerned by intercountry adoption enjoys safeguards and standards equivalent to those existing in the case of national adoption;
  (d) take all appropriate measures to ensure that, in intercountry adoption. the placement does not result in improper financial gain for those involved in it;
  (e) promote, where appropriate, the objectives of this article by concluding bilateral or multilateral arrangements or agreements. and endeavour, within this framework, to ensure that the placement of the child in another country is carried out by competent authorities or organs.

Article 22: Refugee children

1. States Parties shall take appropriate measures to ensure that a child who is seeking refugee status or who is considered a refugee in accordance with applicable international or domestic law and procedures shall, whether unaccompanied or accompanied by his or her parents or by any other person, receive appropriate protection and humanitarian assistance in the enjoyment of applicable rights set forth in this Convention and in other international human rights or humanitarian instruments to which the said States are Parties.

2. For this purpose, States Parties shall provide. as they consider appropriate. co-operation in any efforts by the United Nations and other competent inter-governmental organizations or non-governmental organizations co-operating with the United Nations to protect and assist such a child and to trace the parents or other members of the family of any refugee child in order to obtain information necessary for reunification with his or her family. In cases where no parents or other members of the family can be found, the child shall be accorded the same protection as any other child permanently or temporarily deprived of his or her family environment for any reason, as set forth in the present Convention.

Article 23: Handicapped children

1. States Parties recognize that a mentally or physically disabled child should enjoy a full and decent life, in conditions which ensure dignity, promote self-reliance, and facilitate the child's active participation in the community.

2. States Parties recognize the right of the disabled child to special care and shall encourage and ensure the extension. subject to available resources. to the eligible child and those responsible for his or her care, of assistance for which application is made and which is appropriate to the child's condition and to the circumstances of the parents or others caring for the child.

3. Recognizing the special needs of a disabled child. assistance extended in accordance with paragraph 2 shall be provided free of charge, whenever possible. taking into account the financial resources of the parents or others caring for the child, and shall be designed to ensure that the disabled child has effective access to and receives education, training, health care services, rehabilitation services. preparation for employment and recreation opportunities in a manner conducive to the child's achieving the fullest possible social integration and individual development. including his or her cultural and spiritual development.

4. States Parties shall promote in the spirit of international co-operation the exchange of appropriate information in the field of preventive health care and of medical, psychological and functional treatment of disabled

children, including dissemination of and access to information concerning methods of rehabilitation education and vocational services. with the aim of enabling States Parties to improve their capabilities and skills and to widen their experience in these areas. In this regard. particular account shall be taken of the needs of developing countries.

Article 24: Health and health services
1. States Parties recognize the right of the child to the enjoyment of the highest attainable standard of health and to facilities for the treatment of illness and rehabilitation of health. States Parties shall strive to ensure that no child is deprived of his or her right of access to such health care services.
2. States Parties shall pursue full implementation of this right and, in particular, shall take appropriate measures:

   (a) to diminish infant and child mortality,
   (b) to ensure the provision of necessary medical assistance and health care to all children with emphasis on the development of primary health care.
   (c) to combat disease and malnutrition including within the framework of primary health care. through *inter alia* the application of readily available technology and through the provision of adequate nutritious foods and clean drinking water, taking into consideration the dangers and risks of environmental pollution,
   (d) to ensure appropriate pre- and post-natal health care for mothers,
   (e) to ensure that all segments of society, in particular parents and children. are informed, have access to education and are supported in the use of. basic knowledge of child health and nutrition, the advantages of breast-feeding, hygiene and environmental sanitation and the prevention of accidents.
   (f) to develop preventive health care, guidance for parents. and family planning education and services.

3. States Parties shall take all effective and appropriate measures with a view to abolishing traditional practices prejudicial to the health of children.
4. States Parties undertake to promote and encourage international co-operation with a view to achieving progressively the full realization of the right recognized in this article. In this regard. particular account shall be taken of the needs of developing countries.

Article 25: Periodic review of placement
States Parties recognize the right of a child who has been placed by the competent authorities for the purposes of care, protection, or treatment of

his or her physical or mental health, to a periodic review of the treatment provided to the child and all other circumstances relevant to his or her placement.

Article 26: Social security

1. States Parties shall recognize for every child the right to benefit from social security, including social insurance, and shall take the necessary measures to achieve the full realization of this right in accordance with their national law.
2. The benefits should, where appropriate, be granted taking into account the resources and the circumstances of the child and persons having responsibility for the maintenance of the child as well as any other consideration relevant to an application for benefits made by or on behalf of the child.

Article 27: Standard of living

1. States Parties recognize the right of every child to a standard of living adequate for the child's physical, mental, spiritual, moral and social development.
2. The parent(s) or other responsible for the child have the primary responsibility to secure, within their abilities and financial capacities, the conditions of living necessary for the child's development.
3. States Parties in accordance with national conditions and within their means shall take appropriate measures to assist parents and other responsible for the child to implement this right and shall in case of need provide material assistance and support programmes, particularly with regard to nutrition, clothing and housing.
4. States Parties shall take all appropriate measures to secure the recovery of maintenance for the child from the parents or other persons having financial responsibility for the child, both within the State Party and from abroad. In particular, where the person having financial responsibility for the child lives in a State different from that of the child, States Parties shall promote the accession to international agreements or the conclusion of such agreements as well as the making of other appropriate arrangements.

Article 28: Education

1. States Parties recognize the right of the child to education, and with a view to achieving this right progressively and on the basis of equal opportunity, they shall, in particular:

   (a) make primary education compulsory and available free to all:
   (b) encourage the development of different forms of secondary education, including general and vocational education, make them

available and accessible to every child, and take appropriate measures such as the introduction of free education and offering financial assistance in case of need;

(c) make higher education accessible to all on the basis of capacity by every appropriate means;

(d) make educational and vocational information and guidance available and accessible to all children;

(e) take measures to encourage regular attendance at schools and the reduction of drop-out rates.

2. States Parties shall take all appropriate measures to ensure that school discipline is administered in a manner consistent with the child's human dignity and in conformity with the present Convention.

3. States Parties shall promote and encourage international co-operation in matters relating to education, in particular with a view to contributing to the elimination of ignorance and illiteracy throughout the world and facilitating access to scientific and technical knowledge and modern teaching methods. In this regard, particular account shall be taken of the needs of developing countries.

Article 29: Aims of education

1. States Parties agree that the education of the child shall be directed to:

(a) the development of the child's personality, talents and mental and physical abilities to their fullest potential;

(b) the development of respect for human rights and fundamental freedoms, and for the principles enshrined in the Charter of the United Nations;

(c) the development of respect for the child's parents, his or her own cultural identity, language and values, for the national values of the country in which the child is living, the country from which he or she may originate, and for civilizations different from his or her own;

(d) the preparation of the child for responsible life in a free society, in the spirit of understanding, peace, tolerance, equality of sexes, and friendship among all peoples, ethnic, national and religious groups and persons of indigenous origin;

(e) the development of respect for the natural environment.

2. No part of this article or article 28 shall be construed so as to interfere with the liberty of individuals and bodies to establish and direct educational institutions, subject always to the observance of the principles set forth in paragraph 1 of this article and to the requirements that the

education given in such institutions shall conform to such minimum standards as may be laid down by the State.

Article 30: Children of minorities or indigenous populations

In those States in which ethnic, religious or linguistic minorities or persons of indigenous origin exist, a child belonging to such a minority or who is indigenous shall not be denied the right, in community with other members of his or her group, to enjoy his or her own culture, to profess and practice his or her own religion, or to use his or her own language.

Article 31: Leisure, recreation and cultural activities

1. States Parties recognize the right of the child to rest and leisure, to engage in play and recreational activities appropriate to the age of the child and to participate freely in cultural life and the arts.
2. States Parties shall take legislative, administrative, social and educational measures to ensure the implementation of this article. To this end, and having regard to the relevant provisions of other international instruments, States Parties shall in particular:

   (a) provide for a minimum age or minimum ages for admission to employment;
   (b) provide for appropriate regulation of the hours and conditions of employment; and
   (c) provide for appropriate penalties or other sanctions to ensure the effective enforcement of this article.

Article 32: Child labour

1. States Parties recognize the right of the child to be protected from economic exploitation and from performing any work that is likely to be hazardous or to interfere with the child's education, or to be harmful to the child's health or physical, mental, spiritual, moral or social development.
2. States Parties shall take legislative, administrative, social and educational measures to ensure the implementation of this article. To this end, and having regard to the relevant provisions of other international instruments, States Parties shall in particular:

   (a) provide for a minimum age or minimum ages for admissions to employment;
   (b) provide for appropriate regulation of the hours and conditions of employment; and
   (c) provide for appropriate penalties or other sanctions to ensure the effective enforcement of this article.

Article 33: Drug abuse
States Parties shall take all appropriate measures, including legislative, administrative, social and educational measures, to protect children from the illicit use of narcotic drugs and psychotropic substances as defined in the relevant international treaties, and to prevent the use of children in the illicit production and trafficking of such substances.

Article 34: Sexual exploitation
States Parties undertake to protect the child from all forms of sexual exploitation and sexual abuse. For these purposes States Parties shall in particular take all appropriate national, bilateral and multilateral measures to prevent:

(a) the inducement or coercion of a child to engage in any unlawful sexual activity;

(b) the exploitative use of children in prostitution or other unlawful sexual practices;

(c) the exploitative use of children in pornographic performances and materials.

Article 35: Sale, trafficking and abduction
States Parties shall take all appropriate national, bilateral and multilateral measures to prevent the abduction, the sale of or traffic in children for any purpose or in any form.

Article 36: Other forms of exploitation
States Parties shall protect the child against all other forms of exploitation prejudicial to any aspects of the child's welfare.

Article 37: Torture and deprivation of liberty
States Parties shall ensure that:

(a) no child shall be subjected to torture or other cruel, inhuman or degrading treatment or punishment. Neither capital punishment nor life imprisonment without possibility of release shall be imposed for offenses committed by persons below 18 years of age;

(b) no child shall be deprived of his or her liberty unlawfully or arbitrarily. The arrest, detention or imprisonment of a child shall be in conformity with the law and shall be used only as a measure of last resort and for the shortest appropriate period of time:

(c) every child deprived of liberty shall be treated with humanity and respect for the inherent dignity of the human person, and in a manner which takes into account the needs of persons of their age. In particular every child deprived of liberty shall be separated from adults unless it is considered in the child's best interest not to do so and shall have

the right to maintain contact with his or her family through correspondence and visits, save in exceptional circumstances;
(d) every child deprived of his or her liberty shall have the right to prompt access to legal and other appropriate assistance as well as the right to challenge the legality of the deprivation of his or her liberty before a court or other competent, independent and impartial authority and to a prompt decision on any such action.

Article 38: Armed conflicts

1. States Parties undertake to respect and to ensure respect for rules of international humanitarian law applicable to them in armed conflicts which are relevant to the child.
2. States Parties shall take all feasible measures to ensure that persons who have not attained the age of 15 years do not take a direct part in hostilities.
3. States Parties shall refrain from recruiting any person who has not attained the age of 15 years into their armed forces. In recruiting among those persons who have attained the age of 15 years but who have not attained the age of 18 years, States Parties shall endeavour to give priority to those who are oldest.
4. In accordance with their obligations under international humanitarian law to protect the civilian population in armed conflicts, States Parties shall take all feasible measures to ensure protection and care of children who are affected by an armed conflict.

Article 39: Rehabilitative care

States Parties shall take all appropriate measures to promote physical and psychological recovery and social re-integration of a child victim of: any form of neglect, exploitation, or abuse; torture or any other form of cruel, inhuman or degrading treatment or punishment; or armed conflicts. Such recovery and re-integration shall take place in an environment which fosters the health, self-respect and dignity of the child.

Article 40: Administration of juvenile justice

1. States Parties recognize the right of every child alleged as, accused of, or recognized as having infringed the penal law, to be treated in a manner consistent with the promotion of the child's sense of dignity and worth, which reinforces the child's respect for the human rights and fundamental freedoms of others and which takes into account the child's age and the desirability of promoting the child's re-integration and the child's assuming a constructive role in society.
2. To this end, and having regard to the relevant provisions of international instruments, States Parties shall, in particular, ensure that:

(a) No child shall be alleged as, be accused of, or recognized as having infringed the penal law by reason of acts or omissions which were not prohibited by national or international law at the time they were committed;

(b) Every child alleged as or accused of having infringed the penal law has at least the following guarantees:

i) to be presumed innocent until proven guilty according to law;

ii) to be informed promptly and directly of the charges against him or her, and if appropriate through his or her parents or legal guardian, and to have legal or other appropriate assistance in the preparation and presentation of his or her defence:

iii) to have the matter determined without delay by a competent, independent and impartial authority or judicial body in a fair hearing according to law, in the presence of legal or other appropriate assistance and, unless it is considered not to be in the best interest of the child, in particular, taking into account his or her age or situation, his or her parents or legal guardians;

iv) not to be compelled to give testimony or to confess guilt; to examine or have examined adverse witnesses and to obtain the participation and examination of witnesses on his or her behalf under conditions of equality;

v) if considered to have infringed the penal law, to have this decision and any measures imposed in consequence thereof reviewed by a higher competent, independent and impartial authority or judicial body according to law;

vi) to have the free assistance of an interpreter if the child cannot understand or speak the language used;

vii) to have his or her privacy fully respected at all stages of the proceedings.

3. States Parties shall seek to promote the establishment of laws, procedures, authorities and institutions specifically applicable to children alleged as, accused of, or recognized as having infringed the penal law. and in particular:

(a) the establishment of a minimum age below which children shall be presumed not to have the capacity to infringe the penal law;

(b) whenever appropriate and desirable. measures for dealing with such children without resorting to judicial proceedings, providing that human rights and legal safeguards are fully respected.

4. A variety of dispositions, such as care, guidance and supervision orders; counselling; probation; foster care; education and vocational training programmes and other alternatives to institutional care shall be avail-

able to ensure that children are dealt with in a manner appropriate to their well-being and proportionate both to their circumstances and the offence.

Article 41: Respect for existing standards
Nothing in this Convention shall affect any provisions that are more conducive to the realization of the rights of the child and that may be contained in:

(a) the law or a State Party; or
(b) international law in force for that State.

PART II: IMPLEMENTATION AND ENTRY INTO FORCE

Article 42
States Parties undertake to make the principles and provisions of the Convention widely known, by appropriate and active means, to adults and children alike.

Article 43
1. For the purpose of examining the progress made by States Parties in achieving the realization of the obligations undertaken in the present Convention, there shall be established a Committee on the Rights of the Child, which shall carry out the functions hereinafter provided.
2. The Committee shall consist of 10 experts of high moral standing and recognized competence in the field covered by this Convention. The members of the Committee shall be elected by States Parties from among their nationals and shall serve in their personal capacity, consideration being given to equitable geographical distribution as well as to the principal legal systems.
3. The members of the Committee shall be elected by secret ballot from a list of persons nominated by States Parties. Each State Party may nominate one person from among its own nationals.
4. The initial election to the Committee shall be held no later than six months after the date of the entry into force of the present Convention and thereafter every second year. At least four months before the date of each election, the Secretary General of the United Nations shall address a letter to States Parties inviting them to submit their nominations within two months. The Secretary-General shall subsequently prepare a list in alphabetical order of all persons thus nominated, indicating States Parties which have nominated them. and shall submit it to the States Parties to the present Convention.

5. The elections shall be held at meetings of States Parties convened by the Secretary-General at United Nations Headquarters. At those meetings, for which two-thirds of States Parties shall constitute a quorum, the persons elected to the Committee shall be those who obtain the largest number of votes and an absolute majority of the votes of the representatives of States Parties present and voting.

6. The members of the Committee shall be elected for a term of four years. They shall be eligible for re-election if renominated. The term of five of the members elected at the first election shall expire at the end of two years; immediately after the first election the names of these five members shall be chosen by lot by the Chairman of the meeting.

7. If a member of the Committee dies or resigns or declares that for any other cause he or she can no longer perform the duties of the Committee, the State Party which nominated the member shall appoint another expert from among its nationals to serve for the remainder of the term, subject to the approval of the Committee.

8. The Committee shall establish its own rules of procedure.

9. The Committee shall elect its officers for a period of two years.

10. The meetings of the Committee shall normally be held at the United Nations Headquarters or at any other convenient place as determined by the Committee. The Committee shall normally meet annually. The duration of the meetings of the Committee shall be determined, as reviewed, if necessary, by a meeting of the States Parties to the present Committee, subject to the approval of the General Assembly. The Secretary-General of the United Nations shall provide the necessary staff and facilities for the effective performance of the functions of the Committee under the present Convention.

12. With the approval of the General Assembly, the members of the Committee established under the present Convention shall receive emoluments from the United Nations resources on such terms and conditions as the Assembly may decide.

Article 44

1. States Parties undertake to submit to the Committee, through the Secretary-General of the United Nations, reports on the measures they have adopted which give effect to the rights recognized herein and on the progress made on the enjoyment of those rights:

   (a) within two years of the entry into force of the Committee for the State Party concerned,
   (b) thereafter every five years.

2. Reports made under this article shall indicate factors and difficulties, if

any, affecting the degree of fulfilment of the obligations under the present Convention. Reports shall also contain sufficient information to provide the Committee with a comprehensive understanding of the implementation of the Committee in the country concerned.

3. A State Party which has submitted a comprehensive initial report to the Committee need not in its subsequent reports submitted in accordance with paragraph 1(b) repeat basic information previously provided.

4. The Committee may request from States Parties further information relevant to the implementation of the Convention.

5. The Committee shall submit to the General Assembly of the United Nations through the Economic and Social Council, every two years, reports on its activities.

6. States Parties shall make their reports widely available to the public in their own countries.

Article 45

In order to foster the effective implementation of the Convention and to encourage international co-operation in the field covered by the Convention:

(a) The specialized agencies. UNICEF and other United Nations organs shall be entitled to be represented at the consideration of the implementation of such provisions of the present Convention as fall within the scope of their mandate. The Committee may invite the specialized agencies, UNICEF and other competent bodies as it may consider appropriate to provide expert advice on the implementation of the Convention in areas falling within the scope of their respective mandates. The Committee may invite the specialized agencies, UNICEF and other United Nations organs to submit reports on the implementation of the Convention in areas falling within the scope of their activities.

(b) The Committee shall transmit, as it may consider appropriate, to the specialized agencies, UNICEF and other competent bodies, any reports from States Parties that contain a request, or indicate a need, for technical advice or assistance along with the Committee's observations and suggestions, if any, on these requests or indications.

(c) The Committee may recommend to the General Assembly to request the Secretary-General to undertake on its behalf studies on specific issues relating to the rights of the child.

(d) The Committee may make suggestions and general recommendations based on information received pursuant to articles 44 and 45 of this Convention. Such suggestions and general recommendations shall be transmitted to any State Party concerned and reported to the General Assembly, together with comments, if any, from States Parties.

PART III

Article 46
The present Convention shall be open for signature by all States.

Article 47
The present Convention is subject to ratification. Instruments of ratification shall be deposited with the Secretary-General of the United Nations.

Article 48
The present Convention shall remain open for accession by any State. The instruments of accession shall be deposited with the Secretary-General of the United Nations.

Article 49
1. The present Convention shall enter into force on the thirtieth day following the date of deposit with the Secretary-General of the United Nations of the twentieth instrument of ratification or accession.
2. For each State ratifying or acceding to the Convention after the deposit of the twentieth instrument of ratification or accession. the Convention shall enter into force on the thirtieth day after the deposit by such State of its instrument of ratification or accession.

Article 50
1. Any State Party may propose an amendment and file it with the Secretary-General of the United Nations. The Secretary-General shall thereupon communicate the proposed amendment to States Parties with a request that they indicate whether they favour a conference of States Parties for the purpose of considering and voting upon the proposals. In the event that within four months from the date of such communication at least one-third of the States Parties favour such a conference, the Secretary-General shall convene the conference under the auspices of the United Nations. Any amendment adopted by a majority of States Parties present and voting at the conference shall be submitted to the General Assembly of the United Nations for approval.
2. An amendment adopted in accordance with paragraph (1) of this article shall enter into force when it has been approved by the General Assembly of the United Nations and accepted by a two-thirds majority of States Parties.
3. When an amendment enters into force, it shall be binding on those States Parties which have accepted it, other States Parties still being bound by the provisions of this Convention and any earlier amendments which they have accepted.

Article 51
1. The Secretary-General of the United Nations shall receive and circulate to all States the text of reservations made by States at the time of ratification or accession.
2. A reservation incompatible with the object and purpose of the present Convention shall not be permitted.
3. Reservations may be withdrawn at any time by notification to this effect addressed to the Secretary-General of the United Nations who shall then inform all States. Such notification shall take effect on the date on which it is received by the Secretary-General.

Article 52
A State Party may denounce this Convention by written notification to the Secretary-General of the United Nations. Denunciation becomes effective one year after the date of receipt of the notification by the Secretary-General.

Article 53
The Secretary-General of the United Nations is designated as the depositary of the present Convention.

Article 54
The original of the present Convention, of which the Arabic, Chinese, English, French, Russian and Spanish texts are equally authentic, shall be deposited with the Secretary-General of the United Nations.

In witness thereof the undersigned plenipotentiaries. being duly authorized thereto by their respective governments, have signed the present Convention.